TONYA MASTERS LUDWIG

Crowned

A Faith-Filled Guide for GenX Grandparents

Copyright © 2023 by Tonya Masters Ludwig

All rights reserved. No part of this publication may be reproduced, stored or transmitted in any form or by any means, electronic, mechanical, photocopying, recording, scanning, or otherwise without written permission from the publisher. It is illegal to copy this book, post it to a website, or distribute it by any other means without permission.

Tonya Masters Ludwig has no responsibility for the persistence or accuracy of URLs for external or third-party Internet Websites referred to in this publication and does not guarantee that any content on such Websites is, or will remain, accurate or appropriate.

Designations used by companies to distinguish their products are often claimed as trademarks. All brand names and product names used in this book and on its cover are trade names, service marks, trademarks and registered trademarks of their respective owners. The publishers and the book are not associated with any product or vendor mentioned in this book. None of the companies referenced within the book have endorsed the book.

Unless otherwise noted, Scripture taken from the (NASB®) New American Standard Bible®, Copyright© 1960, 1962, 1963, 1968, 1971, 1972, 1973, 1975, 1977, 1995, by The Lockman Foundation. Used by permission. All rights reserved.

Scripture quotations taken from The Holy Bible, New International Version®, NIV®, Copyright© 1973, 1978, 1984, 2011 by Biblica, Inc.® Used by permission. All rights reserved worldwide.

Scripture taken from the New King James Version®, Copyright© 1982 by Thomas Nelson. Used by Permission. All rights reserved.

First edition

ISBN: 9798374222814

This book was professionally typeset on Reedsy. Find out more at reedsy.com

For my grandchildren and God.
My grandchildren have given me the most beautiful crown that I wear with enormous joy.
God gave me my grandchildren, who are my blessing and my hope.

For both, I am eternally grateful and blessed.

Contents

Preface — iii
1 THE CROWN OF THE AGED — 1
2 GENERATION FOUNDATION — 8
3 BABY BLESSING — 15
4 WELCOMING BABY — 22
5 BA-NANA — 28
6 GOD'S FLOCK — 34
7 EVERYTHING IN BETWEEN — 41
8 IDENTITY IN CHRIST — 47
9 PREDESTINED FOR ADOPTION — 54
10 IT'S DIFFERENT HERE — 61
11 THE BEST OFFENSE — 68
12 GRACE & GRACIOUS — 74
13 STEP FORWARD & STAND BACK — 81
14 BLESSED ARE THE PEACEMAKERS — 88
15 WHAT HAPPENS AT NANA'S STAYS AT NANA'S — 95
16 NATURE & NURTURE — 102
17 SPOIL THE CHILD — 109
18 YOU ARE A CHILD OF GOD — 116
19 YOUR FUTURE IS NOW — 123
20 FRUITS OF THE SPIRIT — 131
21 LEGACY — 140
22 HERITAGE — 147
23 TOP TIPS — 154

| 24 PRAYERS FOR YOUR GRANDCHILDREN | 160 |
| *About the Author* | 167 |

Preface

"Grandchildren are the crown of the aged, . . ."
—Proverbs 17:6, NIV

1

THE CROWN OF THE AGED

Grandchildren are the crown of the aged, . . . —Proverbs 17:6, NIV

This is a beautiful scripture. I wish it could have said, "Grandchildren are the crown of the best generation" or "Grandchildren are the crown of the righteous." Anything besides "the aged"!

Yes, we've aged, but it makes us sound ancient. I suppose grandparents were probably around 900 years old in biblical times, so it fits. Them.

Yet, I'll still take that scripture any day because I proudly wear the crown my grandchildren have anointed me with. It's bright and beautiful, and it makes me feel wise. These little people make me feel special and give me a renewed purpose. When you think life has become status quo and stagnant, along comes a brand new life to shake up your whole world in the best way.

I've been a Nana for over a decade, and I have learned much from my grandchildren about myself, life, faith, and humility. I respect all those with way more experience than me and the remarkable stories they have tucked away that may never be shared with a broad audience.

While many have me beat in years of experience, I know that the joy and blessings to be found in being a grandparent are deep and never lost on me.

My grandchildren leave me at a loss for words most times. I'm rapt by who they are - each with unique personalities, dispositions, and ways of relating to others. I'm taken by the beauty of their hearts and the genius of their minds. I'm lifted by the joy that makes it feel like my heart could burst every time I see their precious faces.

I'd be remiss if I didn't mention the pride and awe that I find in watching their parents (one of whom is my very own daughter!) raise them. They are a team in every way, sharing the joy and the struggles of raising humans while balancing work, homeschooling, and household duties, all while staying laser-focused on God as the center of their marriage.

I've watched my daughter, Kailah, incorporate specific aspects of my parenting but primarily curate the methods she has developed with her husband. While it can be affirming and comforting to know there are things she thinks I did so well with her that she continues the tradition, I'm simultaneously impressed with the things she left behind. The things that I wish I wouldn't have done or wish I would have done differently. This is one of the great benefits of new generations. Each one has the opportunity to bring specific parenting methods and family traditions forward and leave undeserving ones behind.

When it comes to our faith, our walk with Christ is consistently strengthened, and I cannot stress enough the spiritual revival that comes with receiving the crown of grandchildren.

A lot of us had a spiritual awakening while parenting our children. When grandchildren arrive, it becomes a more profound dependence on God and a desire to hear from the Holy Spirit. The dynamics in relationships with your children change, and your role in their lives varies. Therefore, your dependence on God to take control is more significant.

This is why the scripture says that grandchildren are a crown to us. We grow closer to God, closer to Heaven, and those little children are responsible for us becoming better stewards and sharers of our faith. It's a natural blooming of faith-filled anticipation of God's work in these children.

Outside the parenting years, where we watched our children grow into adulthood, we were consumed and distracted by our responsibilities to raise good humans. The added pressure caused us to miss some of the magical moments.

As grandparents, we have the gift of margin, foresight, and insight to enjoy every moment and build the legacy we want to offer them.

When it's your turn to receive the crown, are you ready? I know some people who don't want it to happen for a long time, some who have been so prepared they bought a bassinet for their home long before a baby was even a thought, and some who, no matter what the timing is, would never feel it's quite right.

Whether you have a natural gift for being a grandparent or feel like you might have to work at it a little more than others, I know that these bits of wisdom I've learned along the way will help create a fresh outlook on who you are and how you will fit into the formation of this new family in a new generation. You are an essential part of it. Our maker made that known in Proverbs 17:6. Proverbs is a book of wisdom.

I hope that no matter the season you're in when you receive your crown, you will find blessings in the babies, cherished memories made from unexpected moments, and perhaps even a spiritual renewal that happens naturally when a new life enters the world. This is all by God's design; this is how you know He loves you and sees you.

> *Then she called the name of the Lord who spoke to her, "You are a God who sees me"; for she said, "Have I even seen Him here and lived after He saw me?"*—Genesis 16:13

You are a blessing, and you will receive blessings multiplied. From a practical perspective, having grandchildren is one of the best ways to leave our mark on this world. Whether we're teaching them how to ride a bike, reading with them before bedtime, or simply holding them as they drift off to sleep in our arms, every moment spent with these precious little ones is a chance for us to impact their lives.

From the moment their little eyes open in the morning to when they close at night, they bring laughter and fun to our lives. Spending time with them is an absolute delight—full of silliness and laughter and plenty of hugs and cuddles. Whenever we need a pick-me-up or want to enjoy being around others who genuinely care about us, spending time with our grandchildren is precisely what we need to do.

If you're lucky enough to have this wonderful gift in your life, make sure to cherish every moment you spend with them. They are a precious gift to be treasured, hence the crown you receive when they enter your life. Whether you're enjoying their company now or looking forward to their arrival in the future, one thing is for sure: they are indeed a blessing in our lives.

> *Only be careful for yourself and watch over your soul diligently, so that you do not forget the things which your eyes have seen and they do not depart from your heart all the days of your life; but make them known to your sons and your grandsons.*—Deuteronomy 4:9

Scripture shows us that we are expected to learn from our lives and share wisdom with our children and grandchildren. We have a calling to protect our souls, our children's souls, and our grandchildren's souls with the covering of the Holy Spirit, which we receive through faith in Jesus Christ.

I, for one, have spent so much time wishing I had more time in my younger years, but I'd only want that if I could take the wisdom I have now back to those days. Had I recognized all the ways God has called me to live and how I have been meant to fulfill His purpose, I'd be much more prepared for this season of my life. Now I understand that God's purpose for me has made me well-equipped for my influence on my grandchildren.

That old phrase, "Youth is wasted on the young," is a testament that we didn't know enough when we were young. I suppose the beauty of it is that we didn't know what we didn't know. It would have been amazing to have today's wisdom at that age.

What I perceived about family when I was young to what I know about family now is drastically different. I wish I had spent more time getting to know my grandparents, soaking in their wisdom and insights on life. I wish I had asked them to share more stories and dive deeper into who they were.

We have our roles as whatever we are to each person—daughter, sister, cousin, aunt, mother, in-laws, grandmother. Then, more often than I ever expected, our roles became dual. Great-nieces are more like grandchildren; a cousin is more like a sister. An aunt is more like a mom or grandmother. In-laws are more like primary families. Then again, we might have closer relationships with people without blood relations.

Once you become a grandparent, a change overcomes you that causes you to see all children through eyes of protection and love.

Yes, the crown of grandchildren completely changes your life. When you prayerfully approach your new role, consult scripture to learn what God says about it, and remain open to learning rather than assuming you already know everything, you'll receive all the rewards of the crown.

As a noun, a crown is defined as "a reward of victory or a mark of honor"; as a verb: "to invest with dignity" (Merriam-Webster). Throughout your parenting years, you didn't realize that you were working toward more than a cap and gown with your children. Getting them through graduation seems like a crowning achievement for any parent. Graduation is the pinnacle of parenting.

You've worked hard alongside your child to build them into the people they are today. While the achievement isn't the end of parenting, it is the end of a particular parenting season where your role changes. Your relationship with your adult child evolves into one you can't imagine until you're in it. Some of my life's most beautiful moments have been watching my daughter be a mom.

When you receive the crown of grandchildren, it marks a beginning. The most significant beginning is the chance at a closer relationship with God, a more profound dependence on Him, a heightened awareness of His voice, and finding abundant joy in the small blessings.

You can have all this by remaining in God's word, praying to Him and trusting Him with your grandchildren, and pausing to listen to Him. Be open to those moments that lay the groundwork for your grandchildren to experience His presence through you.

Grandchildren are a blessing, and you are a blessing to them! Your wisdom and insight are also a blessing to your children in their new role as parents. You bring experience, knowing them intimately, and having an intuition about their tendencies.

Whether you need to offer encouragement to new parents, take the baby off the hands of a tired mom, or enjoy a sleepover with your grandchildren, you bring value and a unique perspective to both the parents and children.

Grandchildren add love and purpose to everything we do, bringing us so much happiness and joy that it's hard to imagine life before them.

Pray

Lord, guide me to accept the crown of grandchildren gracefully.

It is a blessing for generations to continue beyond me, and I am grateful that I am here to experience and enjoy the beauty of this season of life.

You created me and brought me to this calling as a grandparent, and I trust that you have equipped me to be the light and salt of your word.

My grandchildren deserve this special part of me reserved just for them.

Thank you, Lord, for sending your Holy Spirit to prepare me and help me rise to my purpose.

In the name of Jesus, amen.

2

GENERATION FOUNDATION

Since I'm writing this book primarily for GenX, exploring who we are and why we are so unique in our approach to life and relationships seems fitting. GenX has so many influences that make us the most adaptable and well-rounded of the generations. We have become the most adaptable and evolved generation in history. Each generation's experiences inform their behaviors, beliefs, values, and how they relate to others. When we understand the experiences that shaped the generations, we can show more grace toward each other.

> *A generation goes and a generation comes, But the earth remains forever.*
> —Ecclesiastes 1:4

The Silent Generation, of which my parents were from, created Boomers. Boomers created more Boomers and GenX. GenX created Millenials, GenZ, and even some Gen Alpha. There are exceptions, but this is the general landscape of generations.

GenX's kids span three generations. Not only are we one of the most diverse generations, but we also created three generations of humans who are nothing like us or any generations before us.

The Silent Generation and early Boomers are similar. They are frugal, loyal, resilient, and hard-working people. They are our parents who stayed with the same company for forty years. They had ultra-frugality embedded in their souls because they started life during World War II, slipped into the Great Depression, and followed that up with the coming of age during the Korean War and the Vietnam War.

Despite knowing not much more than war and financial strife, they exhibited the utmost respect for authority—from bosses to law enforcement and even the president, whether or not they agreed with them. They are the ones who established the concept that children should be seen and not heard. They were better at communicating with customers and co-workers than with their families.

Historian, author, and Silent himself, William Manchester, once said that the members of the Silent Generation were "withdrawn, cautious, unimaginative, indifferent, unadventurous, and silent." I'm not at all convinced that Silents were unimaginative. I think every generation is imaginative. Whether or not they pursue the products of their imagination is the actual question. I would guess that if Silents didn't follow the creativity of their minds, it was likely due to their loyalty to tradition and work rather than a lack of innovation.

Silents raised Boomers who perpetuated corporate loyalty and the lack of emotional connection with people. At home, Boomers were quiet, avoiding the tough conversations, and avoided talking about feelings—theirs or ours. Boomers rebelled against authority and launched the free-spirited living that came with the Civil Rights Movement, the sexual revolution, and the second wave of the feminist movement. Interestingly, Silents became enthralled with Boomer radicalism and adopted many of their traits.

The revolutions, movements, and radical approach to life launched by Boomers gave Silents a taste of freedom and fun they'd never known.

As Silents and Boomers became more established with their jobs and families, they developed a higher tolerance for spending, primarily money they didn't have. Credit cards became how these generations could liberate themselves from the poverty of their childhoods, the frugality of their early adulthood, and the tight budgets they'd followed as they married and started their families. Even still, while they became more financially stable and relied on debt to create the life they'd dreamed of, they maintained a mindset of scarcity and hard work.

GenX started out analog, evolved to digital, and slid into virtual, all while raising ourselves, suppressing our emotions, and recognizing that corporate life isn't the end-all-be-all. We're also the generation that likely had more near-death experiences than a person should, and no one cared. We're dreamers and doers, we're corporate, we've dominated the trades, and we embrace entrepreneurship. We work to live rather than live to work, unlike previous generations.

Many of us carried on the Boomer tradition of credit, but we then met Dave Ramsey, and he changed our outlook on how we handle our finances. We're still using credit, but we're more likely to have lower credit balances and pay them off faster.

We had no parental supervision or emotional support, and we lived primarily surrounded by friends and neighbors. Our parents didn't care about school until report cards came out, and then they were super interested in that D in Math. We had less tendency to rebel because we lacked authority at home, and the only other authority we had meaningful contact with were our teachers. But our parents weren't big on communicating with them either, so we continued to lack authority in our lives.

Most of us got cars at ridiculously young ages because it was easier for our parents if we drove ourselves around. They loved and wanted us but couldn't be bothered by our needs. I don't say this out of spite or disappointment. It is what it is. As I said, every generation was molded according to the time in history we were given life. We're all doing the best we can with what we have. It just so happens GenX was built to be resilient, basing most of our choices and decisions on facts instead of feelings, thinking about what's best for others instead of only ourselves, and living by a creed of perpetual youth.

When the digital world arrived, we had no choice but to learn, immerse, and embrace it. Boomers had a choice to avoid getting involved if they didn't want to. The most they had to do was learn email and how to use a computer. Social media, mobile apps, online shopping, and the like are all options for them that they can take or leave. GenX embraced all that and more. Every generation after us has only and will only know a digital world.

My Mom is a Silent who was raised on a farm. My Dad was a Silent/Boomer raised in the city. They had very different upbringings, resulting in different approaches to parenting, work, spending, and life philosophies. Mom was always reserved, and Dad was the adventurer. They were a great complement to each other, but they had important things in common: silence, indifference, and an inability to communicate in a healthy way.

Personal family experiences are as impactful as a person's generation. It gives me a better understanding of how my parents related to each other, us kids, and our extended family. All it takes is a glimpse into the psychology of a person's upbringing to allow grace to well up within you for their experience and the way they lived.

Fortunately, my parents had close-knit families, the importance of which was passed along to us as we grew up. I may not have heard "I love you" very often, but I knew I was loved, wanted, and belonged. I think that's one of the remarkable things about GenX. Despite our lack of affirmations, physical affection, and quality family time, we were strong enough in mind to know our value within our family units.

> *We will not conceal them from their children, But we will tell the generation to come the praises of the Lord, And His power and His wondrous works that He has done.*
>
> —*Psalm 78:4*

GenX embraced the resilience and hard work ethic of Silents and Boomers, but we vowed to raise our children differently. I was raised to be seen and not heard, and so were my parents. I knew I didn't want my child to ever feel like that. I encouraged my child to have opinions and to share them. When I became a mom, I did just that. My daughter and I had very open communication with each other. No subject was off-limits, and I was always honest with her, keeping in mind boundaries to protect her.

Why would I start a book about grandparenting with an exploration of our experiences with our parents and their generational quirks? Understanding where you came from and how your own experiences influenced you will help you understand your approach to parenting which affects your approach to grandparenting. You will be more self-aware, and that creates healthier relationships.

When I was a child in the 70s, we moved from Florida to South Dakota. The only method of communication we had back then was telephone or mail. So, our move created a divide between us kids and our extended family. While Mom and Dad kept close phone contact with our Florida family, we kids weren't included on those calls. My parents took us on family trips back to Florida every summer to spend time with my Granny, aunts, uncles, and cousins.

On the first day of our summer visit, Granny would give me four quarters. I have vivid memories of playing outside and watching her walk out the front door of her house, wearing a floral housedress, the intense heat causing her to subconsciously push her bottom lip out and blow air toward her forehead in an attempt to remain cool. She'd call me over as she stood on that hot sidewalk. She would pinch the quarters between her fingers and press them into my cupped hand and tell me to get what I wanted with it. This was usually a private moment between us. Even as a child, I understood that she felt it was none of my parents' business that she gave me money.

My cousin and I would walk to the gas station down the street and spend our coins on YooHoos. I knew my Granny wasn't well-off and her dollar donation to my summer vacation was worth far more to me than the financial aspect. Today's youth are getting $20 from the tooth fairy, unlimited access to app purchases, and thousands of dollars spent on elite sports clubs. Grandparents are handing over $25 gift cards. We now live in very different times.

In the case of geographic distance between family members, we now have the blessing of so many methods of technology to remain in close contact. Grandparents now have more direct contact options to maintain their relationships with their grandchildren.

Video calls and messaging, along with video games played via wi-fi allow us to play together though we may be in different states. Fortunately, we also know how to use these technologies to keep us connected.

Generations are exponentially different.

My daughter is a Millennial, my step-sons are Millenial and GenZ, and my granddaughters are Gen Alpha. My goal as a parent was to allow my daughter to have a voice, and strong communication with me, to feel loved, and to hear loving words. I raised her to be independent and capable yet value traditional roles. I raised her to know she can do anything, which gives her the freedom and confidence to be exactly who she is today.

As you receive the crown of grandparenting, you'll become acutely aware of your generational experiences. Through that, you'll develop a unique grandparenting style and perhaps even change how you relate to your adult children. You might even create a new, more positive way to connect with *your* parents. You'll pave the way for a beautiful new season of life abundant in respect, love, and inspiration.

One of the best aspects of our GenX nature is our collaborative and entrepreneurial spirit. Our shared experiences have turned into a desire to continue to share, encourage, and boost each other however we can. That's why I wrote this book for you.

We created a new approach to parenting, and we're building a new system for grandparenting. We're mentally younger than those before us in this season of life. It's not retirement time for us. We feel like we'll always be in our prime and have many opportunities to create a life and a legacy through entrepreneurship and living our way.

We're not like our grandparents or our children's grandparents. Too much has changed. We have evolved in ways others can't fathom. Collectively, we've changed the landscape of life. Now, let's wear the crown of grandparenting in the way that only GenX can.

Pray

Dear God, there's a lot that comes with being GenX. My life experiences are deeply instilled in me and inform my opinions and beliefs.

Thank you for seeing me for who you made me to be. I have raised an amazing child who will be a fantastic parent.

What a blessing to watch generations upon generations being created. It humbles me to know that I'm part of forming the future.

Lord, thank you for my beautiful life. You have provided for me in ways that I could never have imagined.

I am so excited for this new season as a grandparent. I ask that you provide good health and protection for my family.

In Jesus' name, I pray, amen.

3

BABY BLESSING

Grandparents. We all have them, but not all of us will become one. If you're reading this, you've received the crown of grandchildren, or you will soon. Being a grandparent is an indescribable reward in this season of life. Of course, we love our children; we doted on them, nurtured them, and stood by in amazement at their outstanding accomplishments as they grew into adulthood.

But those babies born of someone else yet still hold your blood in their veins? They are a different kind of special. You're about to launch a distinct type of doting. Even though we've all heard how they're so great because you can send them home, I promise you, you will have days you never want to send them home. They change you for the better. A betterment that you don't want to lose touch with.

Being part of GenX means we're highly aware of our youth and age. Much in the way parenthood came at unexpected times and ages for many of us; we were too young, too old, or unprepared in a laundry list of ways. But we did it, we made it through, and we didn't completely ruin our kids' lives. Right?

We still look fantastic and young. Our minds tell us we're still twenty-seven. We might be excited about grandbabies, but do we want that title yet?

Our children having children happens in a lot of ways. They got married and started a family in the most traditional way, or they are single, and the pregnancy is unplanned, or they've been with their significant other for six years but still haven't married, or they met last week, and circumstances are the least ideal. There could be worse circumstances, and there could be better circumstances. Whatever the circumstances, the result is the same: a baby is coming.

Some of us are ready, and some of us get the wind knocked out of us.

Here we are, our babies are having babies, and it seems surreal. Even if the pregnancy announcement doesn't come with fanfare and immediate excitement, it's still a reason to celebrate. A beautiful blessing is about to come into your life.

Pregnancy can be difficult in even the most ideal situations, so regardless of how you feel about the pregnancy, remember that no woman needs to hear negativity toward her situation. Anytime a baby is conceived in not-so-ideal circumstances, the immediate reaction usually comes from image and reputation. What will my parents think of their granddaughter getting pregnant out of wedlock? What will our Pastor and congregation think? How could she ruin her life like this? This baby is going to ruin her college career and her professional career; it's going to stop her from pursuing her dreams and accomplishing her goals. This guy she's with is an idiot and can't hold a job, much less raise a baby. She's been with him for six years, and he hasn't committed. Will he feel trapped now?

Even in ideal circumstances, you may secretly wonder if they're truly ready to be parents. It's a lifelong commitment and comes with a multitude of ups and downs.

All of those questions and anxieties are moot points.

> As you do not know the path of the wind, or how the body is formed in a mother's womb, so you cannot understand the work of God, the Maker of all things.
> —*Ecclesiastes 11:5, NIV*

God makes every single one of us, and He *does not* make mistakes. Read that again. Read that line as often as possible to understand God's power. I believe we achieve full wisdom once we know that we *cannot* understand the work of God. I love that word . . .

Cannot.

It doesn't say we *will* not understand because that would indicate a refusal on our part or an unwillingness to try to understand God's incredible works. It doesn't say we *shall* not understand because that would imply that we could, but we've decided that we shouldn't. The Bible says we *cannot* understand the work of God because we are not made to understand the heights of His ability or the making of His plans. Our brains can learn and understand and retain a lot of information, but the work of God? No, that is definitely out of our grasp to understand.

How does it make any sense that a sperm and an egg—two microscopic globs of gel—mash together and, in a matter of forty weeks, form a living, breathing, thinking, functioning human—an actual person—that walks this earth and changes people's lives? It *doesn't* make sense.

If you think about it, we absolutely cannot understand it, just like we cannot understand how God was able to make the heavens and the earth and the animals and every single plant and insect and all the things that inhabit the world. We cannot understand it, yet He did it. He is the Maker of all things, including the baby joining your family under whatever circumstance God chose. Rejoice! Receive the blessing that God would choose your family for this baby.

My first granddaughter was conceived soon after her parents started dating. My daughter and her now-husband told us about the pregnancy on Valentine's Day. The day of celebrating love. After the shock wore off, we had all those everyday conversations about finances and prenatal care, and we knew that beyond the circumstances, this baby would be a blessing. This year, they will celebrate twelve years of marriage and three children—all girls! When I look back on that uncertain time, I know it was all from God. Based on all the other circumstances in my daughter's life and the timing of this baby, God was at work, and that baby girl changed every single one of us for the better.

Indeed, the news of a baby on the way can be met with mixed emotions. On the one hand, you may feel overjoyed at becoming a grandparent. But on the other hand, you may feel apprehensive about all the changes that are to come. The scripture from Ecclesiastes is worthy of meditating on. No matter the circumstances, there is peace in finding humility and seeing everyone involved as fellow children of God who deserve grace.

Becoming a grandparent is an enriching experience. You might be afraid of what it means for your child even if their circumstances are ideal. Being a parent is the most significant responsibility we face in life. Are they ready for a baby? Can they afford a baby? How will they manage? Are they equipped emotionally and resourcefully to have a baby?

Since all children are planned by God, becoming a parent is a calling, and God equips the called. Trust that God has not created a burden but a blessing. Trust that when a woman is called to motherhood, He does not leave her. Understand that there is not one person in this world whose life happened perfectly according to their plans. This is where your support and guidance come in for your children. You might even need to help them navigate the responses of other family members while gracefully handling your own.

The new parents might need your help in various ways, and it becomes a way for all of you to grow closer and develop deeper relationships with each other.

Our lives go according to God's plans for each of us, including the blessing responsible for the new crown you wear. He created this new life, and you will develop an extraordinary relationship with your child, who is now a parent.

You will be amazed by the relationship between you and your grandchildren. Grand means *foremost* and *wonderful*. Relish this! You put in the work to raise good humans. Trust that you did your job and enjoy the unique position this places you in as a grandparent. The link between you and that baby is foremost and wonderful. If you've spent some time already as a grandparent, you know exactly what I'm talking about. If the baby is on the way, you'll soon find out.

You'll be able to share your wisdom and life experiences with your grandchildren. In a strange turn of events, your grandchildren want to spend time with you and are interested in what you have to say. Remember when your children didn't want to hang around you and thought you didn't know anything? Somehow, grandchildren don't apply that to their grandparents. It's as though a natural reverence in them allows this special relationship to be built.

These principles apply to adopted grandchildren as well. Taking care of orphans is a calling God places on the hearts of those He created for that purpose. Whether you await the birth of a baby within your family or the arrival of a new child in need of a home, your *calling* is all the same, and your crown fits perfectly in any situation.

You will learn from your child's parenting style when you watch your child as a parent. You're in for a wake-up call when you think your kids will handle all their responsibilities as a parent as you did. Praise God for that! Most of us did the best we could, and we made decisions based on our upbringing—the things we'd keep and apply to our parenting style and things we vowed we'd never do to our children. Your kids are going to do the same thing. You can provide much-needed support to your child as they transition into parenthood for the first time.

> *"See that you do not look down on one of these little ones; for I say to you that their angels in heaven continually see the face of My Father who is in heaven."*—Matthew 18:10

This scripture from the Book of Matthew precedes a more popular verse, Matthew 18:11, that many people have heard. This verse has a depth that needs to get more attention and understanding. It tells us that all children have angels in Heaven who watch over them and always see God's face. They see God's face because they are in Heaven, with God, protecting the children. This is how valuable children are to God. God is omnipresent and loves everyone; He can easily watch over them. And He does, but He also enlists angel armies to be on watch for the little ones. If you're ever feeling overwhelmed about a baby on the way or unsure of what the future holds, look back on this scripture. God's already there with His angels and His power overseeing every child's future.

As your family gains another member, renewed relationships may develop. It can encourage healing of past hurts, understanding another's life experiences and allowing everyone to bond when there may have been some emotional or physical distance.

A baby is a blessing that gives a new perspective on everything. It makes you rethink your values, your priorities, and your goals. Newborns hold a lot of power, and they wield it most gently. Becoming a grandparent is a fantastic milestone in life. With patience and understanding, you can help make this exciting transition as smooth as possible for everyone involved!

Pray

Father, give me your eyes to see new life from your perspective. A child, made in your image, will soon join our family. Even if I'm not ready, I know that your timing and purpose for this baby are perfect. Guide me to be supportive, loving, and joyful so my child knows my love is unconditional. Our family is blessed to grow, and you have made this gift possible.

Father, I ask that you keep my family in your loving arms, that your Holy Spirit guides me as I begin new relationships with my adult child and my grandchildren, and that a renewed spirit and love of family will be poured out on us all.

Thank you, Lord, for choosing me as this baby's grandparent and equipping me with extra love to share as our family grows.

In the Holy Name of Jesus, I pray, amen.

4

WELCOMING BABY

When you think about how much things have changed over the years on the day a woman gives birth, it's a little entertaining. Back in the day, fathers stayed in the waiting room, pacing the floors to learn the news of their child's arrival and to finally learn whether they had a boy or girl. Eventually, fathers made their way into the delivery room, allowing them to be the first to share the news of the baby's arrival with grandparents, aunts, and uncles who filled the waiting room.

When my daughter gave birth to her first, it wasn't typical. Her husband, my mom, and I were in the labor and delivery room. Her in-laws from California joined via video on a laptop strategically placed in the corner of the room, allowing them to be present for the birth without compromising my daughter's privacy. My girl does not like to make anyone feel left out.

The decision as to who is in the room at the time of delivery is the woman's decision and must be respected. It's the most memorable moment to happen to a woman, and she should do it in a way that makes her happy and at peace.

> *But the fruit of the Spirit is love, joy, peace, patience, kindness, goodness, faithfulness, gentleness, self-control; against such things there is no law.* —Galatians 5:22-23

Our primary focus throughout this guide is on these fruits of the Holy Spirit. This is an excellent time to highlight them because these fruits will help you in all situations, as a grandparent, and in life. When you can apply any one of these in whatever situation you need, they will make a big difference in how you react, respond, and whether you do at all. The fruits of the Spirit are God's quick tips for positive relationships.

When I had my daughter, I was pregnant until I went into labor, and then I went to the hospital and gave birth on her time. Probably most of us GenX women did it this way.

Now, women can choose the day they want to deliver, and they might choose this for various reasons. They also might choose my method, or they might give birth at home, in a pool, or under other circumstances that you don't understand. When your daughter or daughter-in-law talks about her vision for delivery day, listen, ask questions to understand more, and leave it at that.

If you have concerns about the delivery method, it's okay to address them. Still, I think you should do it diplomatically, be open-minded to their reasoning, and ensure that you only have the best interests of them and your grandchild in mind. It's a difficult spot to find yourself in. You have many genuine fears and uncertainty when your baby is having a baby. This is probably the first moment you truly need to find that place of trust that they're making the best decision for them and that God will be there through it all.

My daughter chose to be induced several days before her delivery date with each child. I supported those decisions each time, and her mother-in-law was against those decisions. Were her mother-in-law and I to battle over our differing opinions and threw my daughter in the middle to choose a side, it would have been unfair and unpleasant to do that to her. Instead, she made a decision that her husband supported, and that's all I needed to know. Also, the control freak in me was into knowing exactly when she would go into labor.

Philippians 4:13 should be on the walls in every delivery room, whether that room is traditional or non-traditional. Wouldn't any woman want to be reminded that she has been given the strength of God himself to endure labor?

Let's face it, giving birth *can* be scary. Yes, it's an exciting time, but the process can be terrifying. Reminders that you can do anything when the strength of God fills your being are transformative. No matter who is in the room or how it's happening, our one responsibility is to pray the Holy Spirit into that room and speak life into the healthy delivery of a precious blessing that's making its way into the world.

You must support their birth plan, even if those plans differ from what you would choose for yourself. Focus on providing emotional support, listening to their fears and concerns, and helping them work through them in a way that helps them achieve their ideal birth plan.

Help them research the options they're considering. If you spend some time learning more about their choices and sharing that with them, it will go a long way in making them feel validated and more confident. The key here is that you don't only point out negative information to sway them toward your preference.

Overall, the most important thing to remember is that it's their baby, and they get to decide how they want labor and delivery to go, barring unforeseen circumstances. Your support can help them feel confident in their choices so that they can focus on welcoming their little one into the world.

For those who will spend time in the waiting room or at home waiting for a phone call, the moment the news of the baby's arrival is announced, it's likely to get frantic. Every single person wants to see and hold the baby, check on momma, and have time to meet the newest member of the family. Hold on. Let's all take a moment to breathe for a second. All twenty-four of you can't pile into the delivery room at one time. Even if you physically can, mentally, you can't. Mom and Dad can't handle the influx of a bunch of people. I suggest you go in small groups of two or three.

The fact is, someone has to be last. Everyone will get time with the baby, no matter who is first or last. But no one's time should be very long. Mom has a lot to do, like skin-to-skin time, getting the baby to latch if she's breastfeeding, and catching up on her rest. Let's never forget she just brought a new human into the world. Be willing to give her space to enjoy these first new moments with her husband and baby.

It's helpful to talk about this before delivery day. Could you find out what Mom and Dad prefer as far as visitors immediately after the birth and how long they want them to hang around? It'll be a more peaceful and confident time for everyone if there's a plan. Whether each group gets fifteen minutes, a half hour, or two hours, a plan is always better.

In situations where there's going to be a lot of people chomping at the bit to see the baby, you can use the hierarchy of grandparents, great-grandparents, siblings, aunts & uncles, and then friends. Again, let the parents take the lead.

If you're not the one in the room during delivery, double-check to make sure that you're time there is okay or if they want to change the visiting times in any way.

Of course, if there are complications, all these plans go out the window so that the care of mom and baby is the priority no matter what.

Pro-tip: Never, ever rush to social media to be the first to post pics or even announcements of the pregnancy, the baby's birth, or milestones.

Those are for the parents. Once they post, feel free to follow, but never be the first. If another family member is the first, that's their battle, not yours.

I will forever be amazed at how social media rules inhabit our lives in the most intimate moments. With the faux pas, the interactions, and the sharing of too much information, it's almost impossible to do it right. Letting them be first is almost always the best option.

As the new family makes their way home, keep open communication about their needs. First and foremost, plan to give them space for the first few days at home unless they'd like to have a gathering that day. Mom's mom might stay with them for a few days, or they might want to go it on their own. You can drop off a meal or let them figure it out. If the new mom is on her own, ask if you can bring meals and offer to help with laundry or kitchen cleanup because any extra help is going to be a Godsend.

As family events, outings, and general life continues, the new parents may be apprehensive about venturing out with the baby. Reassure them that it's okay to take the baby into the world with logical precautions for keeping them germ-free and safe. It's easy to want to stay home and revel in their precious new life, but it's also essential that they remain involved in family activities.

That said, give them the grace to pick and choose when and how they want to participate. While you want to encourage them to be involved, you also want to respect their need to spend time alone as a family getting to know each other.

You'll probably go crazy wanting to soak up as much baby time as possible, but there will be times when pictures and videos will have to suffice. Welcoming the baby isn't only about love and cuddles; it's also about space, respect, and grace.

The one thing I've tried to keep in mind since becoming a Nana is remaining in peace. As I remember my days of parenting, the one thing that is a worthy focus for all family members is keeping peace at the forefront.

> *Let the peace of Christ, to which you were indeed called in one body, rule in your hearts; and be thankful.*—Colossians 3:15

This scripture helps us to remember we were called to peace and when we are mindful of our peace, our hearts naturally fall into a place of gratitude. Even if we have moments where we feel left out, we can be thankful for the baby, our new roles, and this new season of life. Pursuing peace provides the most welcoming environment for your new grandbaby and helps you focus on what's most important during this time of newness and excitement.

Pray

God, I'm so excited about this new baby! Thank you for blessing us with a new family member.

As a mom, I want everything to be perfect when the baby arrives. As a grandparent, I want to cuddle, snuggle, and love on my new grandchild. I've been looking forward to this moment and find myself wanting to rush into it and savor it at the same time.

I want to be mindful of my child's needs and create an environment they will remember with joy and pride.

Lord, please guide me to focus on their needs. I ask that you send your Holy Spirit to fill me with everything I need to be what this new little family needs when the time comes. Please remind me of the fruits of the Spirit and that applying them in all situations brings out the best for everyone.

Thank you for your grace and mercy over my family.

In Jesus' precious name, I pray, amen.

5

BA-NANA

> *The nations will see your righteousness, And all kings your glory; And you will be called by a new name Which the mouth of the Lord will designate.* —Isaiah 62:2

Growing up, I called my grandmother "Granny." My daughter, nieces, and nephews called my mom and dad "Grandma and Grandpa." After I settled into my coming role of grandmother, I felt way too young to be called Grandma! I would only be forty-one when my granddaughter was born, and as we all know, we GenXers are forever twenty-seven in our minds!

I resolved to come up with a cool grandparent moniker that matched my young vibe. I chose Lola. As modern families go, my grandchildren have a lot of grandparents. They are blessed with my husband, Dan (GranDan) and me (Nana), my daughter's Dad, Gary (Papa) and his wife, Leslie (Gigi), Taylor's mom and dad (Papa and Grandma), and several great-grandparents. After Eliza was born, I signed cards to her as "Lola." I spent months trying to get her to say "Lola" and consecrate my identity to her to ensure she would know who I am and call me by my cool grandparenting name.

One day, when she was around sixteen months old, Eliza called me Nana. I was taken aback because we'd never said "Nana" to her and had no idea how she'd come up with it. No matter because from the first time I heard this name she'd chosen for me, I said, "that's who I am!" I often think God had a hand in this. I needed humility. I needed to be reminded that it doesn't matter if I'm trendy. Whether forty-one or sixty-one, my identity is not found in what others think of me. In a new season of life, I must yield to all that comes with maturing and having a growing family. I am His; He will name me, and it will be perfect.

Now that three little girls call me Nana; I can't imagine anything different. The girls often say, "but Nana," and it sounds like "banana," so we laugh about it, and sometimes I'm called Nana Banana. Sometimes they call me an old Granny. I don't care what they call me. I only care that they know how much I adore them and that they are precious children of God.

Many of my friends have cool grandparenting names, which is fantastic. Whatever we are called, we must respond to the call and put importance on our relationship with these little children and their parents over anything else.

Whether you and your spouse are Granny, Nana, Gigi, Nina, Pippa, Pops, Papa, Grandfather, or anything else, who you are doesn't come from the name. It comes from your role - this unique, remarkable, joy-filled role that has given you a crown of gold.

Your new name, in this instance, is one of the covenants with your grandchild. It is attached to a profound connection between the two of you. Your new name as a grandparent carries meaning. Their safe space, their funny friend, their escape from the usual routine of their own home into a world of freedom that still offers safety. Your name is the first outside relationship they associate with, apart from their mom and dad. There's mommy and daddy, and then there's grandma and grandpa. Never underestimate the importance you have in the life of your grandchild.

It doesn't matter what your grandchildren call you. Once you're ankles deep in baby toys around your house and once again buying baby food to keep on hand, the only thing you will concern yourself with is soaking up time with your grandbaby and developing your bond with them.

Five years from now, it's not going to matter what they call you.

A new viewpoint may help you navigate your new title. Looking at your grandparenting role from a stance of joy found in faith can mean freedom from concerning yourself with this detail.

> *These things I have spoken to you so that My joy may be in you, and that your joy may be made full.* —John 15:11

When your joy is first in Jesus, and you accept the joy He offers you, it's a little easier to grasp the ability to let go of the appearance. The appearance of being seen as old, the assumption that you're no longer the you you've always been, and the pressure to maintain your youth all the while enduring the mass of changes your body is throwing at you that signify your actual age. Our bodies defy us even though we still feel young, and suddenly we're supposed to be called Grandma?

I think it's fear of being seen as old(er) that drives our desire to have an acceptable name that we want our grandchildren to call us. After all, we'll refer to ourselves by that with every social media post featuring our grandchildren and every time we talk to them. Just like when we used to refer to ourselves in the third person as mommy or daddy, we're now Nana or Pops.

For GenX, it's difficult for some of us to admit that we're grandparents, much less let someone call us that . . . in public! The late Eighties are more vivid in our minds than last week. We still know and rock out to every song by hair bands, and we pride ourselves on being tough as nails. We're the latchkey kids who had almost no supervision. We had to function in the workplace pre-internet and post-9/11. I went from typing with carbon paper (the literal "cc") and whiteout to learning how to use an IBM computer in the office.

Our grandparents looked like grandparents way before they should have. What fifty looks like now is different from what fifty looked like when we were growing up. Back then, fifty looked more like eighty. Today, fifty looks more like thirty. So, we are understandably confused when someone now calls us "grandma." Cue the confused look.

This backstory is essential to understanding why many from our generation seek a name that separates and defines us better. We're not the grandparents of old. We're the grandparents of a new age. We're bringing the wisdom and experiences of previous generations and creating a mashup combining them with modern thinking, a new understanding of relationships, and more open communication.

> *I will rejoice and be jubilant in You; I will sing praise to Your name, O Most High.*
> —Psalm 9:2

As we consider this scripture, it shows us that the core of our joy is the Lord. When we praise *His* name, we find our joy and gladness. For me, it's a reminder that no matter what my title is at work, regardless of how other people would describe me or what my grandchildren call me, the Lord's name is the only one to be praised. God has many names, and every one of them recognizes an attribute of His wonders.

We praise Him with every name He has, Yahweh, El Shaddai, Jehova Rapha, and every other name, yet no matter which name we call Him at any moment, our relationship with Him never changes. We are His.

If you've never done it, I encourage you to research all the names of God. A new level of confidence comes from learning more about our Heavenly Father.

In the same way, God gave a new name to Saul, Jacob, Sarai, Abram, and many others; He also gave us a new name for this new season. The scripture referenced at the beginning of this chapter from Isaiah says that "the nations shall see your righteousness." This righteousness is part of your legacy. It's deeper than a name. When I tell someone that I have grandchildren, I feel *righteous*. I feel like I did something right.

It's a stunning realization when you have reached this season of life where someone else did something (your child had a baby), but it has a significant and positive impact on how others see you. It's like the crown is being placed on your head repeatedly, and you never tire of sharing the good news of your grandchildren!

Count it all *joy* that you are crowned and called by any name by your grandchildren. The name you are called doesn't make you any less of a grandparent; it doesn't change the generation you're in or your current season of life. From the most formal Grandmother to the hip Gigi, you're still you.

I have over ten years of grandparenting under my belt, and I wouldn't care if my grandchildren suddenly began calling me Granny or Grandma. My only concern is my relationship with them; what they call me doesn't define me or my relationship with these precious children.

You will be an integral part of your grandchildren's lives. When there are holidays and celebrations, they will see you. When there's an emergency, they will see you. When mommy and daddy have date nights, they will see you. Throughout this book, you'll see the many scriptures dedicated to the importance of grandparents. I pray that you will place more importance on your role than your name.

If you follow me on social media, I'd love for you to share with me if you, too, tried to make a more fabulous name stick that your grandchild turned into something different. I'm sure I'm not the only one with a failed attempt at controlling the narrative and having my cool factor completely flipped on its back. I'm still pretty cool, primarily because I finally recognized that a name doesn't define my identity. My faith defines me. My relationships, nature, and how I relate to my grandchildren are all driven by who God says I am.

Pray

Lord, thank you for blessing me with such a full life. I am still in my prime, active, and living fully in all the years you've created for me.

Over time, my identity has been found in my work, family, friends, and you. In this new season, Lord, I ask that you help me to find my identity in you. Who I am to you is the only fundamental aspect of myself. No matter what my family or co-workers call me, and even what my grandchildren choose to call me, I long to be rooted in the person you have designed me to be.

Father, I pray that as I gracefully settle into my grandparenting role, I can be an example to my precious grandchildren of how to follow you. Beyond everything else, my hope lies in their relationship with you, that they know you and that they know they are precious in your sight.

Lord, use me to help them know you.

In Jesus's Holy name, amen.

6

GOD'S FLOCK

GenX has a unique situation that most Boomers didn't have. They are still raising children at home while older children have married and started their own families. Many of you are both actively a parent and a grandparent.

I have many friends who are still raising children at home and at the same time receiving that crown of grandchildren. My take on this is that we GenXer women became pregnant very young with our first child, married, divorced, and several years later married again, and then had more children when their first child was already in their teens. While the first child ventures out, gets married, and starts having children, you might still have a ten-year-old at home.

This can add stress to the joy of grandparenting. One of my friends in this situation mentioned that she feels torn between being there for her grandbaby and keeping her youngest daughter a priority. Interestingly, you could find yourself managing jealousy from your younger children toward their niece or nephew.

Planning for these visits and the potential for emotions to be out of whack will be vital to keeping harmony in your home. My daughter has always done something called "pre-teaching" with her daughters.

When they plan to go somewhere new, do something new or outside of usual routines, or have a medical appointment, she talks with them a few days ahead to start preparing them. That way, they get time to digest the information, ask questions, and receive gentle answers and reassurance from their parents. I believe the girls are much more well-adjusted about many things because of this practice.

Use pre-teaching to help prepare your young child for the grandchild's visit by letting her know the timeframe of the visit, what your plans are during that time, and what you expect from them during that time. If your child has plans with friends, don't keep them from their normal activities because the baby will be there. Give her that space if she wants to spend more time in her room than with the baby. The less pressure and expectation you put on her, the more accepting and positive she'll be toward the baby.

Perhaps you can encourage your child to spend some time with the baby, but don't make it their priority. Make sure you carve out extra time with your child for fun outings, attend sporting and school events, and encourage their older siblings to attend. As you know, having a family means being a little out of touch with everyone else because there is so much to do, but encourage them to stay connected to their younger siblings whenever they can.

If you want to keep the peace for the younger sibling, avoid jokes about them being a built-in babysitter. Nothing can ruin a tween or teen's feelings about a new baby more than making them feel like they'll be responsible for that little bundle of joy.

> *The Lord's acts of mercy indeed do not end, For His compassions do not fail. They are new every morning; Great is Your faithfulness.—Lamentations 3:22-23*

Developing healthy boundaries is an excellent way to help alleviate these concerns. This will require open communication among all of you. Keep in mind your older child is married and now has their own family. You are not obligated or expected to be available at a moment's notice, nor should you create the idea that you have more responsibility or involvement in their family than you should. You are still raising your own family, so make that your priority.

Because of this, from time to time, you'll likely experience an all-consuming weight over not spending *enough* time with your grandbaby or spending *too much* time with them. This is why I chose Lamentations 3:22-23. We have a great love for our family, but God's great love for us is even more profound, and He shows compassion for us to renew us every day.

This is the most challenging part for most grandparents: figuring out your place in the new family dynamic. Rest assured, conflicts will happen but keep your faith in God's ability to work things out for good and not in *your* ability to make things work.

One of the most challenging but rewarding parts of parenting is trying to balance work commitments and family obligations. In today's busy society, it can often seem like there aren't enough hours to spend with our loved ones while ensuring everything gets done on time. This challenge becomes even more significant when we consider having young children who need attention and supervision or if we've become grandparents and suddenly find ourselves caring for our grandchildren instead of our children.

At these times, it is essential to remember that quality time is just as important as quantity when spending time with your family members. Whether you're a parent or a grandparent, make the most of your precious time with your young children and grandchildren.

If your work schedule allows, try to arrange your hours to coincide with key activities in your children's (or grandchildren's) lives, such as school events and after-school programs. This way, you'll be able to spend more time together and set aside less time for working during those busy periods. For example, you might consider working from home a few days a week (if possible) to better juggle your work and family commitments.

An easy way to make the most of your time with your younger children is to get involved in their activities and hobbies. This shows them that you're interested in what they're doing and provides you with quality time together that you can enjoy. If your child is passionate about sports, why not sign up for coaching duties or volunteer to help at their games?

One of the best things you can do for your children (or grandchildren) is to be present in their lives. In today's fast-paced world, it can be easy to get caught up in our lives and neglect the people who matter most to us. Make an effort to put down your phone and focus on your family members when you're spending time with them. Listen to what they say, ask them about their day, and enjoy each other's company.

Taking care of yourself is essential to be your best for your family. This means making time for some "me time" now and then to relax and recharge. Whether it's taking a few minutes to read your favorite book, getting in a workout at the gym, or simply taking a long bath or nap, find time to do something just for you whenever possible.

> *Therefore, I urge elders among you, as your fellow elder and a witness of the sufferings of Christ, and one who is also a fellow partaker of the glory that is to be revealed: shepherd the flock of God among you, exercising oversight, not under compulsion but voluntarily, according to the will of God; and not with greed but with eagerness; nor yet as domineering over those assigned to your care, but by proving to be examples to the flock.*
> —1 Peter 5:1-3

In the scripture from 1 Peter above, the concept of being an example can apply to your adult children. You must set the tone for the way your younger children will be included so that the new baby doesn't bring seemingly further alienation from the older siblings.

We already know that their sibling marrying or becoming pregnant changed their relationship. The younger child, who was probably the star of the show every day, has faded a little into the background of their older brother or sister's life. Add a new baby to that, and they can feel even further removed from their sibling who once doted on them.

This is a significant relationship change for a child to experience. Life goes on, and you're there for them, but their status has taken a major blow. You may have to remind the older one to make extra efforts to spend time with their younger sibling, reach out to them often, and include them in plans when possible.

As a parent, it's an excellent opportunity to start conversations with your younger child and allow them to freely share without being offended if they say something negative about the baby. They're still learning to process their feelings, and you can help them navigate their emotions and reactions.

Be a good listener for your younger kids, and if they're teens, you can offer advice on how they can take an active role in nurturing their relationship with their siblings and nieces/nephews.

If the grandchildren are around, and you're making snacks or hot cocoa, invite your other children to join you. Even if you think they're happy being in their room. Inviting and encouraging them to join is a simple way to ensure they feel included.

Put in a little more effort by inviting your younger ones to go to lunch or yard sales together. You don't have to get super creative or make everything a big event. Your time and attention are the most important things they need.

As I was nearing this chapter's end, I realized that this topic is extremely sensitive and important. I didn't have young children at home when I became a grandparent, so I don't have personal experience in this area. Several friends are currently in this situation and reached out to me for advice.

I hope and pray that the words on these pages are practical guidance that can be helpful. It's a new experience for grandparents and young children that can only be navigated through love, patience, and a willingness to allow honest and open communication. Ensuring younger children have a safe space to be honest about their feelings regarding their experience can be the one thing that helps them the most.

Perhaps, if possible, starting those conversations before the wedding or during the pregnancy can help. While it's likely to be near impossible for them to envision the drastically changed future through dialogue, at least the stage can be set for discussing the coming changes. Let them know it's okay to feel hurt or abandoned but reassure them that they have not been abandoned.

Similar to when people say things at a wedding like, "We didn't lose a daughter; we gained a son." They didn't lose their brother; they gained a sister. From this viewpoint, gain feeds life into them rather than loss. Only God can help us, and them, see the blessings of change. Thankfully we have His word and example to show us how to lead.

Pray

Dear God, thank you for understanding the challenges I face having children at home while also becoming a grandparent.

I want my young children to know they are important and that my new grandchild won't take their place. I know I'll pay special attention to my grandchild, but my connection to my younger children is my priority.

I understand that open communication with my younger children is essential as these new changes in our family come about. Please give me the right words to say at the right time so that I can help my children transition into their new role as an aunt or uncle.

In Jesus' name, amen.

7

EVERYTHING IN BETWEEN

One generation will praise Your works to another, And will declare Your mighty acts.
—Psalm 145:4

You've made it to probably the most challenging season of life: the sandwich generation. Maybe you're taking care of children in some fashion while also taking care of your parents in some manner. You're still working, you probably spend (or want to spend) more time with friends, you're likely traveling more, and yet you have a lot of responsibilities and concerns that tie you down. If your health isn't causing you a headache, it's likely your parents' health is beginning to show wear and tear. Maybe you're vacillating between parent, grandparent, and caregiver roles. That's enough to exhaust a person, but add in your job and other responsibilities, and you're likely asking yourself how you got to this point in life.

You'll have moments when you've planned a sleepover with the littles, and your Dad calls you to take him to the hospital. Your mom will become too frail to clean her house, and you'll have to give up your

Saturday afternoon ice cream date with your grandson so you can help her. And then it's going to flip. Your mom wants you to take her shopping, but your granddaughter has a basketball game, and you intend to keep your pledge never to miss a game. Your Dad's doctor's appointment is at the same time as a meeting with an out-of-town client, so your Mom will have to pick up the slack and drive him.

There will be many days when you'll feel like you're being pulled in every direction by everyone you love, and you can't make them all happy. There's one of you, several of them, and the math doesn't make sense. You can't do it all.

> *And do not neglect doing good and sharing, for with such sacrifices God is pleased.*
> *—Hebrews 13:16*

Scripture shows us that God is pleased when we do good. I wanted to remind you of this because when those frustrating and overwhelming days come along, I want you to reflect and know that God sees you and He is *pleased* with you! Especially when you might not receive much appreciation for all you're doing from the people you're doing for, it's nice to know that even if no one notices, God does.

Being in the sandwich generation is a unique experience. It applies to every generation, not just GenX. However, GenX is unique in that not only are we caring for our children and our parents, but we're also involved with our grandchildren. I believe, in general, GenX grandparents are more involved with their grandchildren than any generation before us. Of course, there are families with multi-generational home lives and grandparents raising their grandchildren as their own, which has happened in all generations.

We want to be there for all the moments and have a vital role in our grandchildren's upbringing and influence. It's a different level of involvement. I'm not saying that previous generations weren't wonderful grandparents; I'm simply saying that we're different.

GenX has held a standard of doing and experiencing everything differently, and our version of the sandwich generation is no exception. We've been trained from a young age to handle things, keep moving forward, and not complain. I'll point out that on this topic, this isn't about complaining; it's about enlisting help because it's the one area where we will experience the heaviest weight of trying to do it all while also hitting a wall because we'll tend not to be mindful of our stress response to this season of life.

I'm a late sleeper, but I'm a night owl, and I work later. This works for me. I've tried forcing myself to get up before dawn and get more done by eight a.m. than anyone else, but all I did was exhaust myself, and I wasn't happy. I became more productive and motivated when I finally accepted my nature and nurtured my reality. Fortunately, my work and family dynamics allow me to nurture my natural rhythms while being present for others when needed.

Even though I have an unconventional schedule, I can operate according to a set schedule or be flexible and spontaneous as needed.

You might live by the seat of your pants or be a rigid planner, but no matter where you fall on that spectrum, you have to expect the unexpected. Planning and schedules will help, as well as enlisting other family members to help with your parents however they can. Eventually, you might have to hire help like a home care service if you work and can't be on call.

A calendar and some advanced planning will help alleviate obligations and expectations, but it's a lot of pressure for one person to shoulder. This is where we focus a little more on boundaries as self-care.

My take on it is two-fold: 1) honor your true nature, and 2) rest without guilt. We get a lot of pressure to wake up early and stay up late and hustle every minute in between. We live in a social media world where nothing is real, and we're supposed to believe everyone is living their perfect, best life. We're only living our best if we honor who we are and set boundaries that help prevent burnout.

To rest without guilt means to recognize and accept when you need rest and do it without shaming yourself or feeling like you're letting someone down. We all know we have to put the oxygen mask on ourselves first. Sometimes the oxygen mask is an hour of Netflix. Sometimes the oxygen is a walk around the neighborhood. Sometimes the oxygen mask is a drink with a friend after work. Whatever it looks like to you to rest, participate in it because rest is part of life. God rested. What makes you think you can work harder than God?

The first step is to make sure that you have a clear plan. You should sit down with your parents and discuss what they need from you on an ongoing basis. This will help ensure that there aren't any surprises or unexpected requests that come up as time goes on. Knowing what everyone expects from you will make it easier to plan your time and ensure everyone's needs are being met.

Equally important is being respectful of your parent's ability to do things independently. After my Dad passed away, my husband and I started having (almost) nightly dinners with my mom. We can spend time with her during a meal and keep up with all that's going on in her life. Sometimes she makes dinner, and we go to her house; sometimes, we make dinner, and she comes to our house.

Mom does most things on her own, but she does enjoy our help with a few things, like changing air filters in the furnace, swapping batteries in the smoke detectors, and perhaps helping her navigate tax season. Otherwise, she does fine. Even still, it's not enough to exist and do well. I like to make sure she is fulfilled and happy. I encourage her to get out of the house by running errands with me, tagging along with her granddaughters on their outings, or just roaming around a store.

When you have parents who need your help with doctor visits, household help, and meal prep, the overwhelm can happen quickly and is often accompanied by guilt. You're human, and it's normal to feel like handling everything for everyone is too much. Usually, it is too much for one person to take, which is why everything mustn't fall on you.

Don't be afraid to ask for help when you need it. If you have friends or family members willing to pitch in and help, take them up on their offer. It can be challenging to admit that you need assistance, but it's better to ask for it than to try to do everything yourself and end up resentful about the demands on your time and energy. We default to the idea that no one can care for everything the way we do, but they don't need to.

Just because your brother might drop in with a pizza doesn't mean he cannot cover dinner duty one night every week. You might prefer a well-rounded meal for your parents, but they need to be treated to pizza night once in a while.

Another sibling can be tasked with filter and battery changes, and make it your sister's responsibility to stop in twice a week to go through the mail if they need that help. If you happen to be an only child or your siblings don't live nearby, it's even more important to have a plan and a schedule. Perhaps you can also reach out to your church for help.

> *"You shall stand up in the presence of the grayheaded and honor elders, and you shall fear your God; I am the Lord."*—Leviticus 19:32

We're in a time when respect for the aged and standing up for them seems to be waning. Healthcare doesn't honestly care for them, young people don't have time for them, and sometimes, we can resent this turn of events where we need to care for them. But, as Leviticus reminds us when we show respect and stand up for them, we are revering God. We honor our mother and father as we have been called to do our entire lives.

I wish more young people understood the importance of honoring our elderly. Your position between two generations may be a ministry to your younger children concerning caring for the family. Including them could give you extra time together and give them more time to relate to their grandparents.

Your time in the sandwich era may be only a couple of years long, or it could be a decade or more, depending on the ages of your younger children. Take a look at your short-term and long-term commitments and how they tie together.

Pray

Lord, I wasn't ready for this season of life. Taking care of my parents while also taking care of my children is so unexpected. With grandchildren now coming into the picture, I want to be my best for everyone.

Father, grant me patience and gentleness, as I know these are the fruits I will need to take care of everyone and myself. When my patience runs thin, remind me that I have been blessed with a family who loves me and appreciate all I do, even when it doesn't seem like it.

Lord, I know I'm not alone in this. I know there are so many people in this same season of life. More importantly, I'm not alone because you are with me. You sent Jesus to walk with me, guide me, and be my friend when I feel no one cares. You've always known exactly what I need in every season of life.

Thank you for remaining near me and allowing me to feel your presence and peace.

In the beautiful name of Jesus, I pray, amen.

8

IDENTITY IN CHRIST

Someone very special to me requested that I address a topic that can, unfortunately, concern mixed-race families: how to navigate public perception with grandchildren of mixed races.

> *Therefore, accept one another, just as Christ also accepted us, for the glory of God.*
> —Romans 15:7

It saddens me that this is even a concern, alas…here we are. In addition to the scripture above, we also know that God made mankind in His image. Everyone on earth represents God regardless of our skin color, nationality, culture, political leanings, or gender. Jesus loves every person, and He came to save every person. It's a sad reality that not everyone subscribes to this fair and just and right thinking. We live in a world where we can't control anyone else's opinions or tongue.

Yet, you still need a practical approach to this earth-bound issue. Not everyone follows Jesus, not everyone was raised right, and sometimes even though people are raised right and follow Jesus, they can still be shockingly ignorant. Whether the couple is of mixed race/culture, adopts a child of a different culture/race, or has multiple children who are all different, some peace can be found in planning for the ignorant. My top recommendation is to consult the parents about how they plan to navigate it and follow their lead. This is an issue that is very personal and is based on individual experiences. There is no standard response. A few questions you can ask to help prepare you from the standpoint of respecting other cultures or backgrounds include: Will cultural customs be practiced? If so, learn about those customs and how you can respectfully incorporate them. Will conversations take place with their children as they get older, or will they choose to live life and not give power to the opinions of others? I've always loved that quote that what other people think of you is none of your business.

Learn about the activities, celebrations, and holidays that are customary to the culture that will be new to you. Participate in them. Be respectful of them. You might have cultural or faith-based practices that are different from theirs. You'll want them to participate and respect yours, too, and it will be a great way to deepen your connections.

Consider other aspects you'll want to learn. Does your grandchild need a different kind of hair or skin care than you're used to? Ask about it, show interest, and know how to take care of it when the child is with you.

Learning everything you can makes you and your family better equipped to respond to outside inquiries.

You can change the narrative every time the opportunity arises, and it will occur. Likely more often than you expect because, as mentioned, people are ignorant. Expect some of those ignorant people to be related to you. When you plan to cut off snide remarks, insensitive questions, and unwanted opinions, you can simultaneously preserve your typical good nature and your relationship with the offender. I recommend something along the lines of, "Our family has been perfectly designed," "Love needs no explanation," "It's of no consequence," or "God made each of us in His image." Whatever your line, immediately move on to a conversation about the other person. They'll forget all about you and your beautiful family.

Concern yourself with loving your family, protecting them from the ignorant, and respecting and celebrating cultural differences. I pray that this doesn't ever have to be a conversation because humanity is sacred, and I pray that people will open their eyes to that truth.

> *The Lord's bond-servant must not be quarrelsome, but be kind to all, skillful in teaching, patient when wronged, with gentleness correcting those who are in opposition, if perhaps God may grant them repentance leading to the knowledge of the truth,*
> *—2 Timothy 2:24–25*

If you have grandchildren of mixed race, you may find that it requires extra effort to create a welcoming environment for all family members. This can be especially true if some relatives are culturally insensitive or even hostile to the idea of multiracial families. However, with some planning and sensitivity, you can help create an environment where everyone feels valued and respected.

The verse from 2 Timothy above instructs us to correct with gentleness. To "correct" others certainly sounds intimidating because we don't want to go around correcting adults in a fashion that feels like we're parenting them or teaching them a lesson. And yet, this scripture advises precisely those actions. If we remember to teach and correct with gentleness, we may have a more profound and lasting effect on others. Gentleness requires respect and kindness. It needs us to be conversational rather than confrontational.

By developing these skills, we create a more diplomatic mindset. You may even be surprised at how much more peace you have when you know you're called to respond with gentleness. It removes the desire for control and conflict. It moves us to accept that we do what we can, but others must take responsibility for their opinions, actions, and impressions.

Is there a history of prejudice in your family against people different from them? If so, it's important to acknowledge these issues, even if they seem painful at first—doing so will make it easier to address them directly as you create plans for your multiracial grandchildren.

When you acknowledge a family presence of prejudice, you can break the prejudice pattern. Generational patterns can only continue as long as each generation participates in abuse, addiction, wrong-thinking, judgemental behavior, etc. You may come from generations of people with prejudicial tendencies, but it can, and should, end with you.

Even if you cut it off in your own nuclear family, but you have a sibling who continues to perpetuate it, you'll have removed it from your line so that your children and your children's children no longer have to suffer with unloving and hurtful messages of hating others.

Once you have considered these issues, it's time to begin implementing changes in your home life that will allow all family members to feel more comfortable. Be conscious of language and speech patterns when speaking with others. People from different cultures have different expectations or ideas about what is polite and respectful. Communicating effectively with everyone means acknowledging these differences rather than pretending they don't exist.

Try to be willing to engage in honest talks about how you can best respect the new culture. It might be awkward initially, but your vulnerability will most likely be appreciated.

> *For the kingdom of God is not in words, but in power. What do you desire? That I come to you with a rod, or with love and a spirit of gentleness?* —1 Corinthians 4:20–21

IDENTITY IN CHRIST

Implementing the spirit of Gentleness when cutting off generational patterns will show spiritual maturity and personal growth to others. Keeping our tendencies in check and remaining disciplined can be challenging when we depart from faith or spiritual practices. It can be a slow process, but slow is better than nothing. As you move, you may inspire others to do the same. When your growth is slow and intentional versus fast and significant, you avoid blindsiding people who aren't used to this side of you. The thing is, becoming a grandparent brings this side out pretty quickly.

I've been a Christian my whole life, became more committed to my walk with Christ while raising my daughter, and went all in as a grandparent.

For GenX, it seems this is how many of us have evolved and grown into our faith walk. Thank God for children because I shudder to think where many of us would be today if it weren't for them.

Fortunately, we're an open and accepting generation, but it's possible just as many of us took the opposite route due to family influence. This is why we need to be willing to examine our hearts and belief systems, have those difficult conversations, and perhaps even step out of our comfort zone by venturing into a space we may not know much about.

> *and He made from one man every nation of mankind to live on all the face of the earth, having determined their appointed times and the boundaries of their habitation, that they would seek God, if perhaps they might feel around for Him and find Him, though He is not far from each one of us; for in Him we live and move and exist, as even some of your own poets have said, 'For we also are His descendants.'* —Acts 17:26-28

The truth is the truth is the truth. "He made from *one* man *every nation* of mankind . . ." He made Adam in His image; therefore, every person is a child of God. Every child of God has value, purpose, and impact.

I listened to a podcast recently, and the guest shared that he had been reading books on the end times and beliefs of other cultures to help himself gain a better understanding of their views, which also allowed him to see not only how we're different as Christians, but also how similar we are despite our varied views.

It was a great lesson in recognizing that we spend so much time focused on what makes us different when we could focus on what makes us all the same. Each of us belongs to the human race. We'll be better off if value is placed on our humanity instead of political affiliations, culture, or other aspects that don't matter. I don't think anyone comes to the end of their life wishing they'd made one more argument for their political party's sake. Unfortunately, we may be tasked with reminding people we love that negativity doesn't have a place in our homes.

Making your home a welcoming space for all cultures doesn't have to be complicated – but it requires effort and intentionality if you haven't experienced it throughout your life. By creating an environment where everyone feels respected and valued, you can ensure that your grandchildren grow up proud of their heritage.

Pray

Lord, it's easy for me to forget that I am your child. Thank you for this reminder that when I look at my children and grandchildren, I see them the way you see me, with unconditional love, pride, admiration, and grace that's unending.

No matter what our family looks like now or in the future, I pray that every member will be met with acceptance and support from everyone they meet. Lord, I ask that you equip me to end any generational patterns that deny that you are the image in which each of us was created.

I pray your Holy Spirit will provide the gentleness and self-control I need to respond and guide lovingly to bring deep understanding and healing.

You are the Lord of all.

In Jesus' Holy name, I pray, amen.

9

PREDESTINED FOR ADOPTION

If your child has been called to adoption, be prayerful and helpful however you can, as this is a decision no one enters lightly. Whether God calls them or they've chosen adoption due to infertility, it's their family journey, and a grandchild is on the way. The child may be an infant or 12 years old, but all that matters is that every child deserves love and a chance at a good life and a safe home.

You can play an essential role in helping your child navigate the adoption process. Adoption is a calling, and even though it may not have been your calling, you can support your child as they pursue the plan God has for them.

If you are feeling trepidation about adoption, it's okay to feel that way. Maybe you never felt a tug on your heart to adopt. Perhaps you fear the unknown. There are a lot of unknowns, like health, behavioral, and cultural concerns, among others. Integrating a child into your family in a way you've never experienced before is a lot like . . . becoming a parent for the first time.

Most of what you might fear with an adopted child could have happened or happened when you had your first child. Honestly, those concerns come up with every child. We can't know everything we might encounter, whether we welcome a biological or adopted child. Adoption is an extraordinary and highly personal journey for those who choose or are called to this path. For some, it may be something never considered, and it might instill deep dread and fear, and some believe it's the one thing they were put on this earth to do.

> *And whoever receives one such child in My name, receives Me;—Matthew 18:5*

The Lord has called all of us to adoption in some sense. The widowed, the elderly, and the abandoned. I have a role with my great-nieces as their Nana. Without diving into family dynamics, the bottom line is it was more important that they experience their relationship with me as Nana instead of Aunt. It's a blessing that I can be present, fill a void, and offer the assurance that I am theirs no matter what.

When we open ourselves to adoption—whatever that looks like—we open ourselves to answer God's call and fulfill His plans. My parents opened their home to several people while I was growing up, not through official adoption but through providing a safe place, food, guidance, and acceptance whenever the need arose.

If you're unfamiliar with the adoption process, take some time to learn more about it. This will help you better understand what your child will go through and how you can best support them. Ask if you're unsure what they need or how you can help. I believe the one thing they need the most is a listening ear and a shoulder to cry on as they navigate the ups and downs of the adoption journey.

Be supportive as they face the range of emotions they'll experience through the process. Remember, it's their calling, not yours. Encourage them even if it hurts you to see them hurting. You may be concerned for them as they experience excitement, fear, anxiety, or even sadness. You must be there for them emotionally, no matter their feelings. Let them know that you love and support them unconditionally.

Help them navigate the paperwork to help reduce their stress and make the process go more smoothly. The adoption process can involve a lot of paperwork. They might need to rely on you for the past ten addresses they've lived at or to remind them of specific details required for their application. Sometimes those conversations can offer a little walk down memory lane that will warm your heart.

There are many resources available to help people who are adopting a child. Please help your child connect with these resources to get the necessary information and support. For example, if they're adopting a newborn, is there a breast milk bank in their city that they can contact to help the baby get the best healthy start?

Helping your adult children prepare for the adoption of a child is a meaningful way to show your love and support. Remember that the adoption process can be challenging, but with the support of family, it's enriching. Being supportive will help make this time even more special for your entire family.

Adoption day is unforgettable for both the adoptive parents and the child. If you're able, be there to share on the joyous occasion. It's a moment that your child will remember for the rest of their life.

> *He predestined us to adoption as sons and daughters through Jesus Christ to Himself, according to the good pleasure of His will,—Ephesians 1:5*

We are all adopted in some way. Literally and figuratively, by the families of our close friends, by our churches, and by God. Has the lack of a blood relationship ever prevented you from forming a close and unbreakable bond with someone? Probably not.

As you become a grandparent, the best thing you can do is recognize yourself as a lifelong learner. Future generations are going to do something you've never dared. Go along for the ride. Choose hope, choose love, and choose life. Only good can come from those things.

There are many ways you can help your family welcome adopted children. Not all of these suggestions will apply to every family, and some of them may not apply at all. Either way, you'll have more insight to make this a positive experience for the rest of the family.

Suppose your adopted grandchild is from another country or a different cultural background. In that case, it's essential to ensure your other family members understand what the child may go through—and how they can help.

Children who are displaced from the culture or country they were born into should be given extensive grace. While they're adapting to their new family and surroundings, you can also learn about where they came from and the unique conditions of their former home.

You can learn about your adopted grandchild's culture (if it's different from yours) and share that information with other family members.

Frequent check-ins with your children and consistent communication with other family members will be helpful during the adoption process and when the child comes home. The fewer surprises there are about the child or the coming home plan, the better off the child will be, and the better off other family members will be, so they aren't taken off guard by anything.

If you still have children at home, spend time helping them learn about the new child on the way and give them some ideas on how they can connect with and get to know their new niece or nephew. Becoming an aunt or uncle at a young age can be challenging, and when you add in the adoption aspect, they will need extra attention.

Your younger children might enjoy learning about holiday customs, celebrations, or religious practices from the adopted child's culture. Help them incorporate some of those cultural aspects into your celebrations and holidays. This can be a beautiful way to help these children bond with each other and start their relationship with respect for one another that will last a lifetime.

An adopted baby should be treated as if you were present for the nine months of anticipation of their arrival. Likely, you'll be waiting longer than nine months. Even though you may not be in the delivery room for this child, they still hold the same place in your life as one born of your flesh.

In the case of an older child adopted into your family, developing a relationship with them will require a different type of effort and time. This is natural and also applies to your child who adopted them. Look to your child for guidance on navigating this getting-to-know-you time.

Since they've likely gone through classes and received education and guidance on welcoming a new child into their home, they will also have helpful information for you as the new grandparent. Rely on them and trust that their methods are the best for both the child and you.

As of the writing of this book, my daughter and her husband are preparing their family to welcome children through foster care with the intent to adopt. As a mom, I have felt every emotion about this. As a Christian, I've felt guilty for some of my feelings about it. Fear and doubt don't have a place in Christian hearts. Accurate as that may be, I'm sharing the truth about my experience of my child's adoption journey.

I've had days I want to beg her and her husband to let their little family of five be. They're perfect and have such a beautiful rhythm to their life and such peace in their home.

Yet, none of that will change when they adopt a baby. Babies are the epitome of beauty and peace. The only thing that will change is the amount of beauty and peace because it will increase.

I can't wait for this new baby to be blessed by my daughter and her family. My heart swells with joy when I think about the incredible family waiting to welcome this baby. That child has no idea what's in store for them. But I do. Three amazing sisters who are intelligent, faithful, and empathetic. A mom whose heart has never known any boundaries for love, who has a gift for gentleness, and who keeps her home in peace. A dad who is insightful and giving, who provides the best childhood moments that become beloved childhood memories. He's built two treehouses by hand, by himself!

Despite any fear or doubt, I trust God, know my daughter's intuitive capabilities, and I will love unconditionally. I will teach them about everything from reading to starting a business.

The baby we have yet to welcome through adoption will receive the gift of the playful, adventurous heart of their GranDan, who will instill a pursuit of faith in their life. They will also be blessed by the loud, funny, loving, rowdy, kindhearted, and incredible extended family members who are close-knit and put God and family first.

This scripture below perfectly describes humanity and how each of us falls into the description of adopted children. We are all so different, yet all so very much the same.

> *After these things I looked, and behold, a great multitude which no one could count, from every nation and all the tribes, peoples, and languages, standing before the throne and before the Lamb, clothed in white robes, and palm branches were in their hands;*
> —Revelation 7:9

Pray

Heavenly Father, thank you for adopting me into your Kingdom.

Many days I feel I have no place next to you and have yet to earn the reward of having a beautiful room in your house.

Then you remind me of the children waiting for a forever home. I can't imagine any one of them feeling they have to earn love or that they don't deserve a family. You did for me what my child is doing for them. Thank you for reminding me that I don't have to earn a place with you. Your sacrifice secured my spot. My faith is rewarded because I know you.

Lord, difficulties may come about through the adoption process and afterward. I know you will be with us, loving us through it.

I pray that you will place divine patience and faithfulness over my child as they pursue adopting one of your children.

In the name of Jesus, I pray, amen.

10

IT'S DIFFERENT HERE

The moment my first granddaughter was born, my heart raced out of my body and attached itself to her. I was done. Life became about her, her every move, her every milestone, every glimpse of her personality, all of which brought immeasurable joy.

I was so taken with her that I begged my daughter not to have more children. I was confident there was no way I would be able to love any others as much as I loved her. This shouldn't have come as a surprise because my daughter is an only child, so for me, it made sense that there should be one grandchild for me to invest all of my attention, devotion, and love.

She laughed at me and told me she wanted more than one child because she had no siblings. She felt something missing and wanted a group of siblings so they'd all have someone. (Cue the knife in my heart).

Truthfully, I didn't know she felt that way until that moment. I thought I knew everything about her, and when she shared that with me, I had a tiny bit of regret, but I recovered quickly because I knew that God had never put it on my heart to have another child. His plan was perfect, and I am confident in this.

My daughter has cousins she is very close to who are more like siblings, not to mention many other relatives with whom she has strong bonds, and I have no concerns that she is lacking anything at this stage of her life.

She became pregnant with my second granddaughter when the first was nine months old. I was still a little worried about how I would be able to split my love to cover another child. But when you think of God's love, He has never divided His love among all His children. He increased it to cover all of us the same. And that's what naturally happened to me. Once again, God set the example for how we are to love.

There was no reason to feel I'd be slighting one child to love another. I could amplify my love, increasing it to cover all my grandchildren, and how much richer life would be because of it!

Believe it when you hear that a grandparent's love for a grandchild is different. This isn't a slight to the love we have for our children. It's a different kind of love because we have different types of relationships. Without the pressure of molding a child into a productive citizen, the ability to immerse yourself into your grandchild's childhood, evolving from season to season, and growing into their own person is an incredible and unique experience.

For that friend who wondered if one of her grandchildren would drive her crazy, you can almost guarantee that will happen. The thing is, you see it differently than with your children. When it's your children, you worry and wonder whether they'll always be like that; what if they do these things around other kids and embarrass themselves? What if everyone else finds them annoying? You worry about these things because you are responsible for ensuring they turn out okay.

As a grandparent, all you have to do is love them through it. They act crazy and out of control one day, and it makes you a little insane, but at the same time, you see them for who they are, and you see past

IT'S DIFFERENT HERE

the behaviors to the heart of that precious child, and it doesn't matter how they act because you love them beyond behaviors.

On the other hand, will you have a favorite? Absolutely not. I'll qualify my position by sharing that I don't believe in favorites—Favorite Aunts, favorite cousins, etc. When you label family members as favorites, even jokingly, it leaves a little scar on anyone in earshot. It may not leave a mark that can be seen, but the emotional scar never goes away.

Rather than having favorites, you might identify more with one than another. One is always bound to have a personality similar to yours, and another is bound to be the opposite. The same happens with your spouse, children, siblings, and parents.

Grandchildren are precious and life-changing. They give us respite from the world's craziness and our daily concerns. They remind us to be joyful and grateful and to seek moments where we can be carefree.

My grandchildren challenge me to do more and be more than I would if it weren't for each of them. I've learned and grown as a person, and as I've mentioned, I've grown exponentially in my faith because of them. That is because no matter their personalities or behaviors, they all are children of God. They are faithful and prayerful and show gratitude in ways many adults have a hard time being able to do.

One thing I wasn't prepared for was feeling like I just became a best friend for life. To clarify, I *want* to be their best friend. I know I can be more of a friend to them than their parents can because the nature of our relationship allows for it. More importantly, I want them to feel safe that they can come to me in any time of trouble or worry or fear, or sadness and know that I will keep their confidence.

Little children, let's not love with word or with tongue, but in deed and truth.—1 John 3:18

You can talk about love all you want. You can say "I love you" every day. What do your deeds say? Trustworthiness and faithfulness in the Lord show love in profound ways.

We must be people who make our actions speak louder than our words.

I'm curious what my place will be as far as confiding in me one day - and what they will or will not share (obviously outside of serious issues). As a grandparent, I've found that I want to be everything to them. As they grow up, I can see that they are not creating that natural barrier of independence from me as their mother did when she was their age. It gives me so much joy to experience such a beautiful depth of love that is unique to us.

Our parenting years were filled with joy and drama. Our grandparenting years are primarily joy.

Being more youthful than our grandparents, we have a unique perspective that comes from raising our children differently, which translates into grandparenting differently. While we may not always be able to relate to the challenges of modern parenting, our "old-fashioned" advice, support, and love are still valuable.

> *They will still yield fruit in advanced age; They will be full of sap and very green,*
> *—Psalm 92:14*

The fruit we bear in old age, of course, is our grandchildren. And they will keep us fresh and young at heart. There is so much blessing in scripture about being a grandparent. The importance of grandparents, the renewal of our youthfulness, the strengthening of our faith, and the eternal impact we have on our grandchildren.

The mutual benefits grandparents and grandchildren provide each other are many. The Bible shows us that this relationship is important and valuable. Perhaps some grandparents pull away and give distance to their children when they start having babies. But a family is meant to work differently. We're meant to influence each other and live in community with one another.

There is so much talk about people living in community, yet the focus is never really on families. Impact and ministry begin at home. Share the fruits of who you are with those closest to you so they receive the goodness in you.

Grandparents have the luxury of extending more patience than parents because the thing about age is that wisdom comes with it. We know how it ends. Everything worked out in the end, so we could have spent much less time stressing about the little things.

We also can extend a little more grace than parents. I've said it before, and I'll repeat it, we can be fun and relaxed because we don't have the pressure of making sure these little humans turn out to be good adults. We already know they will be amazing because we raised their parents to be amazing.

> *Let me hear Your faithfulness in the morning, For I trust in You; Teach me the way in which I should walk; For to You I lift up my soul.—Psalm 143:8*

We've covered the importance of giving your adult children space to find their way with their new family, but I want to make it abundantly clear that our adult children still need nurturing. We may not have experienced the same need for nurturing because, as GenXers, we didn't receive much of it growing up. Still, we raised our children in a very nurturing way, resulting in their reliance on us into adulthood for reassurance.

In the Psalm above, these are words lifted to Jesus. We can also apply them to children and parents. Even adult children. Our adult children love us and need us to show them the way once in a while, just like we need reminders that our Heavenly Father's love is steadfast, and we can always turn to Him for guidance.

This is a trickle-down effect when practicing your faith and impacting your children and grandchildren. This love and joy for our grandchildren help us connect deeper to our Father in Heaven, positively impacting our relationship with our adult children and immersing ourselves in our doting grandparenting role.

> *But the mercy of the Lord is from everlasting to everlasting for those who fear Him And His justice to the children's children,* —Psalm 103:17

Fearing and loving the Lord impacts generations upon generations. Fearing and loving the Lord translates into loving our family well. Fearing and loving the Lord brings righteousness to our grandchildren.

We have a beautiful opportunity to not only spoil our grandchildren and love them with all our might, but we also have the blessing of showing them how well we love and respect their mom and dad.

The level of safety, security, and confidence you can instill in your grandchildren when they see positive and loving interactions with their parents is immeasurable. It proves that parents love their children forever, no matter what happens or how much trouble they might get into.

Pray

Lord, thank you for the blessing of being a grandparent. I find genuine joy in my grandchildren and an all-new connection with my child.

Loving my family is not only my calling but my greatest joy. Please send your Holy Spirit to give me gentle nudges when my child may need extra attention. I know I focus so much on my grandchildren, and sometimes I need the reminder that my children still need me, too.

Thank you for the ever-evolving seasons of life. Being a grandparent is such a gift! There is so much more to learn about my grandchildren, and I ask that you help me be fully present when I am with them so that they feel and know in their hearts the love I have for them. May they also feel your love for them through me as I help them get to know you more.

In Jesus' Holy name, amen.

11

THE BEST OFFENSE

You have been a fantastic mom. Your children adore you because you provided them with the right balance of discipline, responsibility, and love. They had a good childhood, they have cherished memories, and they are confident high-functioning adults because of you.

Remember that as they become parents.

Remember that you took the best parts of your parents' style, removed some things they did, added some things they didn't, and created your unique way of parenting that worked well for your family. I'm taking you through this reminder because your children will launch—what seems to be—a full assault on your ability to be a responsible adult.

You might be spending a day with your daughter and grandbaby, and when leaving a store, you secure the baby into his car seat in the way his mommy taught you to from day one. You walk around the car to get in and realize momma came along behind you to double-check that all straps are in the proper position and that all mechanisms have clicked into place.

Take a moment.

We both know your first instinct was to be offended that your own daughter didn't trust you to buckle the baby in properly. I strongly encourage and implore you to replace that thought with something like, "I'm so proud that I raised her to be such a conscientious person. It's helped her to be a great mom."

See what we did there? Instead of being offended, we recognized that your child is a good parent. The most important thing we're doing is ensuring the baby is safe. You did the buckling, and she double-checked; the baby is good to go.

Let me make something abundantly clear in this scenario: your daughter did not double-check the straps and buckles because she didn't trust you. She checked them because her momma brain needed reassurance that her baby was safe.

You remember what it was like as a new mom. Hyper-aware and hyper-fearful and just plain hyper sometimes. You being an experienced parent doesn't make her any more seasoned. She needs to do these things and learn and grow through her parenting season the way you did.

Looking back on my journey as a Nana, I had plenty of opportunities to be offended, and I even took some of them. Eventually, I realized I didn't need to be offended. I needed to take comfort that my daughter was mindful and bold in ensuring her children were properly cared for.

Offense is an emotion created by Satan to destroy relationships. If you have not read *The Bait of Satan* by John Bevere, read that next after you finish this book. If Satan can ensure that you are offended often, that will ensure you are isolated from those you love, giving him more leverage in your life.

The best defense to offense is awareness. Recognize when you feel offended, and don't say one word until you change the narrative around the situation. I say this consistently throughout our time together: unless the baby is in danger, try your best to determine whether the advice is needed and maybe even ask if your input is wanted. If your advice isn't desired, that's okay. Baby is safe, his needs are being met, and he's receiving a lot of love, so all is well. Right?

> For God has not given us a spirit of timidity, but of power and love and discipline.
> —2 Timothy 1:7

Yes, all is well. In another chapter, we discuss wanting to guide our children in their parenting journey. Still, the offense issue is of concern in this grandparenting season and every relationship.

In this relationship, it's essential to be aware that if your child double-checks the car seat or prepares their baby's food differently than how you did for them, or if they require the use of certain items rather than the ones you use in your own home, it's not a time to be offended.

The parents' requests and requirements for caring for their baby aren't about you; it's about the baby. Let's face it, parents today are much more informed about products, risks, and best practices than we were. Our children have mom groups on Facebook, millions of sources of information on the interwebs, and the methods they created based on knowledge of their child, all of which inform their opinions and decisions.

All we had was what our parents did, followed by books on parenting which maybe some of you read (I didn't). I did a lot of things differently than my parents. I did a lot of the same things my parents did. I don't know if they were ever offended by the things I did differently. If they were, they didn't say it out loud.

As a parent, it's easy to get offended when someone questions your choices. As a grandparent, it's easy to get offended when your children don't take your advice or even want it.

We intend to be helpful when we offer advice or share tips, and it's usually not because we see something done wrong. We want to share our approach in case it could be helpful. It's the human condition to want to help and share our experiences for the benefit of others. Isn't it interesting that it can lead to hurt feelings when we want to be helpful to those closest to us?

It's almost like taking a step back and working your way forward again during this grandparenting season. You must develop a new respect for your child and their spouse to set the boundaries for a harmonious relationship. I know this seems counterintuitive to what you envisioned for this time in your life, but trust that it will all work out for the best for your entire family.

The opportunities for offense to pop up are limitless. From the car seat moment to clothing choices, food and feeding, and even toys, there are shockingly many times that differing viewpoints will be raised, and not one of them is "right." They're just different. Our perspectives and choices come down to what we feel are best for us based on our knowledge and goals.

When you prepare a bottle for the baby, and mom or dad wants to check the temperature of the milk before you start feeding him, don't be offended. Please take a moment to be thankful that they know to do this. Thank them for double-checking, and proceed to feed the baby.

I used to get upset that my daughter wouldn't get clothes at yard sales rather than buying them new. I can't count how often I pointed out that children grow too quickly to spend a lot of money on clothing and shoes. Nevertheless, she'd buy new clothes. Eventually, she started going to the big community consignment sales and shops, mixing the gently used with the new. Did it matter where she bought the clothes? Not at all. I just wanted to see her save money by not buying new. These little things aren't worth being upset about.

You can offer your best tips for feeding, bathing, and bedtime shortcuts; when they do the opposite, you can let it go. You can choose not to be offended or hurt because they didn't choose your way. They aren't rejecting you; they're choosing their way. Seeing how my daughter and her husband's intuition for their children has shaped their parenting makes me so proud of them.

GenX parents sought ways to be efficient and quick and keep moving. We raised Millenials who are more intentional and more likely to live in the moment and take their time. We raised them to be this way, so it's not sensical to be offended by their take on parenting.

GenXers are experts in being offended. It's our toxic trait. We're strong in our opinions and values and will not be swayed. We get offended because we worked for our place in life. Who we are and how we think was earned through self-sufficiency, self-raising, and a little self-loathing. When someone wants to judge us or debate us, we get some fight in us.

> *One who is slow to anger is better than the mighty, And one who rules his spirit, than one who captures a city.* —Proverbs 16:32

When you realize we share the goal of love and protection for the baby, removing offense from your arsenal is easier. Lack of offense leads to closer bonding with your adult children. It allows you to take a step forward again, but this time with boundaries that benefit everyone.

Boundaries may seem like a blocker to close relationships, but they are the one thing that makes them healthy. They can also help us avoid the downfall of offense. I'm not saying that it's not okay to feel your feelings. I'm simply suggesting that if we look at these moments from a place of love and good intent, we are better equipped to preserve our feelings and avoid being offended over something not intended to offend.

Offense is an emotion that leads to barriers in relationships. Barriers are not the same as boundaries. Barriers are like a wall, blocking our ability to communicate and share experiences. Boundaries are like thin lines that allow us to share experiences without expectation. They offer us protection while we are vulnerable because they are born out of respect for one another.

I hope you won't take the bait of offense, but if you do, you have the tools to recover quickly and place the relationship over being right.

> *You know this, my beloved brothers and sisters. Now everyone must be quick to hear, slow to speak, and slow to anger;—James 1:19*

Think about good, noble, pure, and praiseworthy things because what we think is what we become. When we change our thoughts, we change our impact on those around us—most importantly, our children and grandchildren.

Pray

Dear God, thank you for these reminders to resist being offended. It's natural for me to want to help or offer what I believe are better ways or helpful tips, but I don't want it to be interpreted as being distrustful. When I share my advice, please remind me to be gentle and kind, keeping my relationship with my child top of mind instead of the need to be right.

Please help me recognize when my worry or anxiety is coming out in a way that might make my child question their confidence and ability to be a good parent. Thank you for watching over my family, keeping them safe, and giving me grace.

In the precious name of Jesus, I pray, amen.

12

GRACE & GRACIOUS

> *nor yet as domineering over those assigned to your care, but by proving to be examples to the flock.* — 1 Peter 5:3

Please keep your hands to yourself unless they ask you for one. Oh boy, it took me a minute to learn this one. Many thoughts, emotions, and worries enter the picture when your baby has a baby. You want things to be easy for them, and you want to pass along words of wisdom that will make them one day tell all their friends that they would never have made it as a parent without their mom and if, like me, you're a control freak, you probably have convinced yourself that if they do it your way, everything will be fine.

Trust their parenting. Things are not done the way you did when you had your kids, which is probably for the best. God gives us an innate ability to connect to our children and understand them as no one else can. Guess what? That includes your child and their children. Unless there is something that requires concern, like post-partum depression, a rare situation of detachment, or God-forbid abuse by a parent, you must allow them to get to know their baby and develop their parenting style.

As I began to sit back and watch my daughter and her husband evolve into their roles as mom and dad, I developed an intuition for knowing when they needed my guidance and when I needed to be a calm presence. I learned to wait and watch and see if they would ask for my help or my opinion. If they didn't, my goal was to keep my mouth shut. I'm not saying I was, or currently am, perfect at this, but I try very hard.

You may think the baby should be eating solid foods sooner, weaning from the breast, potty training, or crawling, walking, and talking sooner. Please don't say these things out loud. Your child is doing the best they can and is most likely doing what's best for their baby with the intimate knowledge they have of this little human's abilities and growth.

If you live close to your children, healthy boundaries are a MUST. This rule applies to both sides. While you might assume they want you to come over daily to help with the baby, make sure you ask. While the new parents are learning how to take care of this new life and your help is welcome, they're also navigating their new family dynamic, and they must be given that time and opportunity to do so without you around all the time. Be mindful, offer your presence, but don't be offended if they say they don't need you.

If you live far away, don't automatically jump to the assumption that you'll be flying out and staying for three weeks. Respectfully ask them when might be a good time for you to be there for them and let them take that wheel. You know your relationship with your child and their spouse. If they would love for you to move to their city and help them daily, maybe you should consider that. Every parent wants something different from the grandparents. The best way to know for sure is to have a conversation.

At the other end of the spectrum, while you might want to have your precious little grandbaby around all the time and welcome them with open arms anytime you can get them, it's essential to keep the balance in your own home. If you still have other children at home, or if you and your spouse are empty-nesters, be mindful of maintaining your routines and lifestyle while making accommodations for your new grandbaby's place in your life.

A delicate balance is to be achieved, and when you do, it creates a beautiful, sweet relationship among all of you. That said, be sure to listen to the cues and be willing to give your kids a break when they need it. As you know, parenting is exhausting. We're never fully prepared or ready for it, and every parent needs a break, no matter how great they are.

You'll know the signs when you see and hear them, and when you do, offer to take the baby for a few hours so mom can nap, take baby overnight so mom and dad can enjoy a quiet dinner together and a night of uninterrupted sleep, or pop in to deep clean the kitchen.

A simple way to measure your verbal contribution is by using the acronym T.H.I.N.K. When you want to contribute a thought or perhaps an instruction or suggestion to their parenting, ask yourself if your contribution is True, Helpful, Important, Necessary, and Kind. Some versions of this attribute the word "Inspiring" to the I in this acronym, but in this situation, Important is more appropriate.

The most *important* word in the acronym is Necessary. Most of the time, you'll view your advice as true, helpful, important, and even kind, but if it's not necessary, then it's best to err on the side of silence.

Unless your kids are doing something that puts the baby in danger or could cause real problems, let them make their choices. We had the luxury of figuring things out on our own, and they deserve the same consideration. It's okay to make mistakes as a parent. We learn, we grow, and we become better. If the issue is simply the difference between how you would do it and how they're doing it, let them be.

Necessary input includes recognizing the onset of illness that perhaps the new parents haven't tuned into yet, recognizing a safety hazard like the baby is starting to crawl and a bookshelf hasn't been anchored to the wall, or developmental milestones unachieved during the first twelve months of life that may indicate an underlying issue.

As your grandchildren grow and gain traction on achieving educational milestones, Do. Not. Compare. Them. To. Anyone. Else. Put the comparisons down and back away slowly. We are always so quick to make comments like, "He should already know how to speak a full sentence," "You already knew how to read by her age," or "Don't you think you should have taught him how to tie his shoes by now? His sister mastered that much earlier."

Again, unless there's a legitimate concern about the development or well-being of the child, let it go. Of course, you want to be helpful and point out potential issues, but it's unnecessary. Lean toward showing support, offer to help work on the milestones with the child, let mom and dad know they're doing great, and remind yourself and them that no two children ever do things at the same time . . . and that's okay.

When we remember to do the time test, it can help alleviate concerns. Is this concern likely to be a concern in a month? A year? Five years? If the answer is yes to a month, that might be okay. If the answer is yes to a year, maybe that's a concern. As the more seasoned one, it's up to you to first discern the time test and then discern whether further conversation is warranted.

Your child will appreciate your advice and guidance at the appropriate times. It never hurts to ask if you can offer input. Most times, they'll welcome it. It's an interesting dynamic between adult children and their parents, especially when babies come along. They don't have all the answers, but often I think they want to appear more knowledgeable than they are for your sake. They don't want you to worry about them or have concerns that they can't handle being a parent.

While their experiences aren't new in the world of parenting, they're new to them. Respecting their opportunity to learn and figure things out on their own is a big way to honor them. Keep in mind that you didn't know everything when you brought your first baby home...no one does. We all figure it out, taking it one day at a time.

We've all probably heard the saying, "There's nothing new under the sun . . . " What many may not know is that this is scripture.

> *What has been, it is what will be, And what has been done, it is what will be done. So there is nothing new under the sun.—Ecclesiastes 1:9*

When you become a grandparent, the truth of this is more meaningful. It equips you with the wisdom you can impart to your children during their parenting season.

We had the same experiences when our children were growing up, but we were in too deep to see that we'd gone through many of the same things ourselves. When you're twice removed, there's a renewed understanding of our own experiences growing up, the experiences raising our children, and then we see them again in our grandchildren.

Remember that this is someone else's time to be a parent. Let the moms and dads do their job. You're the grandparents! You're the fun ones. Be there to guide and advise when you're asked to; otherwise, enjoy yourself and the littles!

There can also be a lot of pressure on grandparents to help out with their grandchildren, whether they live nearby or not. While you may want to be there for your adult children and the new addition to their family, it's essential to find the right balance so that you're not overbearing or making your children feel like they need to do everything themselves.

One way to approach helping out with your grandchildren is simply being present when needed and offering support in whatever way possible. For example, if your child is having difficulty getting used to life as a new parent, you could offer to spend the day simply being present and providing encouragement and support. Or if your grandchild is sick, you could offer to come over and help take care of them so that your child can still go to work or take care of other responsibilities.

Of course, respecting your children's wishes regarding their new family is essential. If they're sending the message that they want to go it alone, then try to respect them and give them the space they need. It's also important to remember that your grandchildren are their children, not yours, so ultimately, it's up to your children when they welcome your input and your time helping them.

You are a blessing through your role as a grandparent. Try to relax and not worry so much about being perfect. Movies, books, and all sorts of ideals feed our imaginations about how a grandparent should interact and show up when grandchildren come along. Just as each child is unique, will achieve milestones on their own time, and have gifts like no one else, you will naturally have a special role formed through time and relational experiences.

The best thing you can do is let them know you're there for them, you want to respect boundaries, give them space to get to know each other, and that you're a call away. Let them know you want to visit anytime you can if that works for them. This way, you are clear about your intent to give them time and that you would not consider it a burden if they ask for your help.

> *But as for you, proclaim the things which are fitting for sound doctrine. Older men are to be temperate, dignified, self-controlled, sound in faith, in love, in perseverance. Older women likewise are to be reverent in their behavior, not malicious gossips nor enslaved*

> to much wine, teaching what is good, so that they may encourage the young women to love their husbands, to love their children, to be sensible, pure, workers at home, kind, being subject to their own husbands, so that the word of God will not be dishonored.
> —Titus 2:1-5

These new relationships are a dance. Be graceful.

Pray

Heavenly Father, I'm entering a beautiful season of life because of your blessings!

When I think of the amazing grace you've given me, I want to return that a thousand times to my family. This is a perfect time to remember that grace is the one thing I can give that doesn't necessarily get noticed. These moments make me feel more connected to you and my new role as a grandparent.

I'm so thankful that with each new stage of life, I'm finding ways to strengthen my relationship with you and my family.

In Jesus' name, I pray, amen.

13

STEP FORWARD & STAND BACK

If you thought you had to work with many mixed messages when they were teenagers, get ready for the influx of mixed messages now that they're parents. Prepare for a lot of changes to come your way. Be open to rolling with the newness so that it's less stressful for everyone when things begin to happen.

Your relationship with your children and their significant others will change. It has to. As GenX parents, many of us cultivated a very different kind of relationship with our children than our parents did for us. We're more communicative with our children, we're closer, we share experiences, and we spend a lot more time together. This can't translate into our children's marriage and family. For most of us, our children became our best friends after they became adults.

Just as you embarked on your own with your own little nuclear family, so your child must also be afforded the same experience. Graciously, positively, and without embitterment.

You will still enjoy a close and beautiful relationship with your adult children. Still, healthy boundaries should be created for the relationship once they have a family.

Just as you had new responsibilities, obligations, and time demands when you started having children, your children are now experiencing the same thing. You had to limit your time with friends and family because a baby takes time, energy, and a learning curve. While you might feel like being around a lot for them means you can help them, I promise you they need time to themselves. They need to get to know each other, develop routines and establish a rhythm for their little family, which doesn't include you daily unless they ask.

Add to that, the last thing you want to do is be the cause of stress on the new parents to do more, feel more obligation to appease you, or make them feel like they have to be running around more than necessary.

The best advice I can give is to put yourself in their shoes. Not what you would do if you were them, but consider your unique children, in their situation, and what's best for them.

My daughter and I are as close as you can imagine. I was a teen when I had her, we practically grew up together, and after she reached adulthood, we naturally became best friends. I intentionally mention "after she reached adulthood" because parents should never be their child's friend. I believe friendship is reserved for when you're done raising them. It never works to be a parent and a friend. Parenting then friendship.

Although your friendship remains in place, you must respect that their spouse comes first, and once the babies start coming, they move you to third in line. All of this is okay! This doesn't mean you're never going to see them.

Fathers, do not antagonize your children, so that they will not become discouraged.
—*Colossians 3:21*

Kailah homeschools her children, and a homeschooling family is a special kind of busy! Homeschooling isn't what the general population believes it to be. Set learning times, co-op classes, sports, friends, and other activities exist. They're on the go a lot, and often the only time I see my daughter is when she drops the kids off or we attend the girls' events. This is the season they're in that is way more important than anything else.

When I've gone as long as I can without seeing them, I call or text and ask if I can come over or tag along while they run errands. It doesn't matter how we spend time together, only that we do.

Another concern involves babysitting. It's appropriate and helpful to offer to take the baby for an evening so the parents can get some time together and focus on their relationship. Being available for a standing day or evening caring for the baby is your call. Remember, healthy boundaries work both ways. It's good to be there for them, and at the same time, it's necessary to ensure that you don't become the constant caretaker.

If you are filling a role of daily care when the parents go back to work, you'll need to decide if that needs to be a paid role or if it's going to be free.

When my oldest granddaughter was born, everyone in the local area worked outside the home except my dad. He was retired by then. He babysat four of his great-granddaughters, which was a pretty good gig. Nothing made him happier than those babies, and it gave him a little "walking around" money. While he wasn't paid at the level of a regular daycare, he was still compensated for his time and consistent availability for the children. It was a beautiful arrangement because the girls could be with family instead of a crowded daycare, and they helped keep my dad active and happy.

Please understand that if you're not in a place to provide daycare for your grandchildren, don't feel guilty about this. Whether it's due to your career or you don't want to be tied down to a child, that is your choice. You earned your time to be free. My daughter is a mental health coach and sees local clients every Thursday. Thursdays are my days with the girls. I don't need to be paid for this—it's one day, I adore my time alone with them, and we have built beautiful relationships because of our time together this one day each week.

They live two blocks away, so we see each other more often than one day per week, but other times are brief visits or perhaps a few hours on a weekend night while my daughter and her husband have a date night, and other times are sleepovers.

Over the years, we've established a routine that works for everyone. You'll figure it out, too. It takes time for everyone to learn their new roles and how you all fit together. You're all still pieces in the same puzzle, but your shapes might have changed a little making it necessary to reconfigure and settle into your new space.

When you become a grandparent, your relationship with your children will change in several ways. Maybe you always took vacations together before the baby's arrival, and now those vacations are no longer a priority. Perhaps you get together frequently, and whenever you want to plan something, the typical response is that they're too tired, don't have the money, or it won't be a good situation for the baby.

It's fine and good that this happens. Don't push. This new family is navigating their way with each other. There's a lot for them to figure out regarding what works for them and what doesn't.

> *But seek first His kingdom and His righteousness, and all these things will be provided to you.*—Matthew 6:33

Does that scripture seem odd? Righteousness? What does this have to do with you not seeing your kids as often as you used to?

We GenXers have tended to put our kids on a pedestal. Made them a sort of idol, if you will. Often, it's not until they get married and start their own families do we get the wake-up call that they are individuals pursuing their own lives. Matthew 6:33 is a reminder that when you seek God first, everything else works out. Even the little things.

You'll realize that God is in everything, and the biggest blessing is that your children and their children are healthy and happy. God is creating a new generation of your family that will impact the world. When you're having a moment because you're not part of their day-to-day lives, remember that this is the way it is supposed to be. You raised your child to be independent and create their own life apart from you.

I'm not saying to let the relationship fall by the wayside, but it will take more work—especially on your part—to keep the relationship going. Remember when you were once in the same season of life and how it was essentially on everyone else to reach out to you if they wanted to see you? Remain faithful, and don't let pride, frustration, or sadness get in the way of your relationships with your adult children. After all, they need you to be the one who can step up because they're doing their most important work right now.

To help maintain a positive and nurturing relationship, make an effort to stay in touch regularly—text before calling or requesting a video call visit. Video calls are underrated because they can give you a real connection when you can't see each other in person.

Continue to invite them to family events and celebrations. Please don't assume they wouldn't want to join. Extend the invitation with grace if they decline. Don't forget about the little things. Sending a thoughtful text will let them know you're thinking of them and that you care about your relationship.

When you do talk to your children, talk about things other than your grandchildren. It's natural and acceptable to want to talk about your grandchildren but make sure you maintain interest in the adults' lives as well.

If you're unsure about what you should do, ask. Instead of wondering whether you should do something, invite them to an event, or request a visit, ask them. This shows respect for boundaries while also letting your wishes be known.

I've seen and heard a lot about grandparents who wait for an invitation to see the baby. If there's one thing I know, this is the biggest mistake that leads to misunderstanding, hurt feelings, and confusion for both sides.

Likely, your kids are expecting you to ask to visit them. Rather than wait for an invitation, could you ask for permission?

If there is any simple thing that will create trust and confidence is to ask and invite. Ask and invite. Ask and invite. And in all things, give grace and be gracious.

When you give them the grace to decline an invitation, you give them confidence that they can trust you not to take "no" personally. When you get a "yes," be gracious. Let them know you appreciate the time you have been given because, often, it affects not only you but others in the family.

Our fourth grandchild was born while I was writing this book. It's incredible to experience every new life that comes and to have a grandchild born while writing this book was pretty special. It reminded me that this time with newborns is exciting but can be overwhelming.

Everyone in the family is so excited to meet the new baby; mom and dad want to keep him from being exposed to too many people (germs, chaos) and interrupted schedules. We all have so much respect for that, but we want what we want. And we want snuggle time with this new precious addition to our family because he's ours.

"Ours" applies to a lot of people, though. Mom's side, Dad's side, steps, halfs, grandparents . . . so many people are seeking a slice of time with this new family member. We want to bond with him.

Isn't that what it's all about? We want to develop a bond and connect.

We want to be known. We want to be loved back, and we want to be valued. Sometimes, we must stay back and give a little distance to create closeness.

Being a grandparent isn't a race for who's first to witness a first. It's not a competition to be the favorite. It's far and wide the ability to give grace and be gracious in all things. As grandparenting teaches us many lessons, it's an incredible blessing to recognize we are in an all-new phase of learning and growing which springs up new life within us.

Pray

Lord, sometimes it seems like a precarious dance to figure out how to navigate all the newness.

Through it all, you will be there to help us create a harmonious way to establish new relationships and boundaries.

Lord, I ask for your guidance and patience as I get to know my new grandchild. I don't want to be overbearing, but I want to spend as much time as possible with my family.

Your way is always perfect, and I trust you will show me the correct times to step forward and the best times to take a step back.

In the name of Jesus, I pray, amen.

14

BLESSED ARE THE PEACEMAKERS

> *"Blessed are the peacemakers, for they will be called sons of God."*—Matthew 5:9

The *"other"* grandparents.

They're not your enemy, and you are the "other" grandparents to them. Sometime, somewhere in the history of grandparents, we became territorial. We turned grandparenting into a competition. We do it better than them. Their house isn't as fun as ours. They don't know the kids/understand the kids/treat the kids as well as we do.

We have a few narratives that are unnecessary and false. Full transparency, I get it. I've been guilty of these narratives. But when they say "it takes a village to raise a child," the truth of that not only lies in the upbringing, protection, and guidance of children, it lies in the variety of personalities and talents that children are exposed to among their many and varied family members.

Of course, they need a protective grandma who never lets them out of sight. They also need the "other" grandma that lets them loose in the yard and allows them to climb the tree and slip a time or two. They need the grandpa who reads to them and imparts wise words and the "other" grandpa who makes them learn how to bait a fishing hook, carry them over their shoulder, and spin them around.

I fall into more of the nervous Nelly type with a life goal to keep those babies close and safe from harm at all costs. My husband is a spontaneous risk-taker who thrives on fun and laughter. I'll let you guess which of us they think is more fun. In our relationship, we have a balance between the two of us for our grandchildren.

Nurturing your grandchildren's relationship with the "others" is a beautiful life lesson to give them. As they grow older, they will see that you value their well-being enough to encourage what's best for them. Your open heart, accepting spirit, and willingness to share them freely will benefit them greatly. The point is when we remember that all people have value and are gifts to those we love, we can enjoy much more peaceful relationships with every generation of the family.

For those who live close to their grandchildren while others live far away, it's even more essential to encourage phone calls, video calls, and simply talking about their other grandparents. This will nurture the kids' relationship with those grandparents while building confidence and trust in you since you are showing approval and acceptance of their other grandparents.

This is especially true when there are strained relationships in the family circles. As long as there is no risk of harm to the children, your role is to be open and accepting instead of territorial and "protective" in situations where protection isn't essential.

Don't sleep on this verse. Blessed are the peacemakers! Being a peacemaker often means giving up your peace to make peace for others. Being a peacemaker is so essential that they are called children of God. Peacemakers don't back away from conflict; they move forward in the quest for righteousness and peace. I could write a complete bible study on this one sentence of scripture, but you get the idea.

Being a peacemaker does not mean being a doormat or allowing lousy behavior. It means being objective, considering both sides of the issue, and providing sound advice or action when things are in a state of conflict or unhealthy behaviors.

A special note to those of you grandparents who don't live near your grandchildren: don't overdo gifts and material things. Of course, gifts are lovely, and children love receiving them. Balance them with handwritten cards mailed with printed photos of you that they can tape to their wall. Mail them a game or craft and have a second one with you so that when you have a video call, you can play a game together or create a craft together. Read a book while mom or dad is rocking them to sleep. Create a scavenger hunt for their parents to set up as you guide them through it during a call.

Get creative with the ways you nurture your relationship with your distant grandchildren. Those sweet little ideas turn into precious moments they'll always treasure. When they visit you, you come to see them; these personal interactions will have established a relationship so that you don't have to start over at each visit.

Speak positively about the grandparents who live near your grandchildren and see them frequently. Creating any disconnect or conflict will only harm the children. Ask about their recent visits and favorite things to do with them, and encourage them to enjoy their time with them. If the other grandparents are awful, find something positive or don't talk about them at all. Eventually, your grandchildren will become adults and see things for themselves, but they'll never forget that you didn't make things awkward for them and that you responded out of a place of love and peace.

Regarding the other grandparents, try not to take sides against your child's spouse and their parents. It's important to remember that your grandchildren love both sets of grandparents, and part of your role is to support your children by helping them maintain unity in their marriage.

Even if you disagree with the other grandparents' choices, being courteous and respectful is essential. After all, they, too, are your grandchildren's grandparents, and they love them just as much as you do.

Instead of complaining about how the other grandparents are doing things differently than you, try seeing their style as a chance to learn from their experience. You might come away with a better understanding of who they are.

Be encouraging about your grandchildren's time with the other grandparents. Encourage them to come up with fun suggestions like visiting the zoo or a museum together. Your support of their time with the other grandparents will help strengthen your relationship and give your grandchildren the freedom to grow in their time with their other grandparents. This kind of support and encouragement will significantly impact their confidence.

When the other grandparents visit, knowing how to handle your time with your grandchildren can be challenging. Even though my grandchildren live very close to me, and I see them frequently, I back off when my son-in-law's family visits. I view this as their time to develop their relationships and create memories. If the visit is a week or longer, I will request to stop by and hug the babies for a little bit because I cannot go a week without seeing them; however, we get along well with his family, so we typically end up having dinner or some other gathering while they're here.

Of course, there are some problematic relationships when you combine different people from different walks of life, but choosing peace is vital to holding everyone together. We're well aware of those who thrive on drama rather than peace—every family has at least one person in that category. As long as boundaries are in place so that the drama is limited and the children are given protection from negativity, that is the primary goal that can make all the difference.

Mom's Side/Dad's Side

Sometimes, the truth hurts. The mom's side of the family will likely see the children and grandchildren more often than the dad's side. I'm not saying it's right or wrong; I'm just stating a fact. This has been the way of the world for as long as I can remember. You will have to work a little harder, get more creative, and make more concessions if your child is the dad.

As the mother of a daughter, I understand that a mother/daughter relationship is a unique bond that essentially creates a magnet between them. It is almost impossible to keep them apart! Let's face reality. In Genesis, God says a man shall leave his father and mother and cleave to his wife. This is biblical, y'all. This means he is meant to go where she goes and stick by her, come what may.

As the mother-in-law of a daughter, I know that her mom gets first dibs on their time. Her mom gets the first option when they need someone to take the baby for any significant period. Even though my stepson's mom and I are in the equation, we take next in line in that order. Mom's mom, Dad's mom, step-mom.

The blessing is that we're all friends, and our relationships are based on kindness and respect for each other. So even though I might be bummed that we aren't first in line for the baby, I know he's in great hands and loved well.

To get your time with the children and children, host Sunday dinner once or twice per month, make ice cream dates once in a while where you bring a bucket of ice cream and a few toppings over to their house, and make sundaes together.

Don't wait for an invitation to visit when there is a new baby. They'll find your skeleton one day with your phone in your hand, waiting for them to call. They are too busy and exhausted to think about anything outside their baby. They are not sitting around charting all the visiting hours for the grandparents, aunts, uncles, cousins, and friends who want to spend time with them. If you're going to see the baby, call and ask to set up a time that works best for them. And do that as often as you want to see the baby. They'll feel good knowing you want to be there even when it's a no.

The flip side of this is that often new parents spend a lot of time at home, so they might be waiting for you to want to visit, but they know you're busy. You're waiting for them to invite you, they're waiting for you to ask, and in the meantime, no baby cuddles are happening. Communication is a beautiful thing.

Regarding holidays, host your holiday time together on a different day than the actual holiday. The day before, the weekend after, whatever works for all of you. My aunt always hosts Thanksgiving for her family the Sunday before Thanksgiving because everyone has somewhere else to be. She still gathers the family together and enjoys the traditional meal, and come Thursday, it's her and the sale ads preparing for all the shopping she can handle.

Like the grandparents separated by distance, remember to be creative and understanding. It's great that your grandchildren are so loved, and so many people desire time with them; make sure those efforts aren't causing stress on the children.

> *If possible, so far as it depends on you, be at peace with all people.* —Romans 12:18

"So far as it depends on you . . ." You cannot control how anyone else behaves, reacts, or speaks. But as far as it depends on you, you can choose peace. I'm human, and I understand that frustration with others can be overwhelming. We're not talking about being perfect; we're striving toward inner peace, which always results in outer peace.

Even when things are rocky, and your patience is limited in the case of the other grandparents or your child's spouse, when you choose to keep peace in your heart, a gentle spirit follows, and grace becomes the experience of those around you.

This type of self-awareness and self-control comes with practice. It's an interesting dynamic being a grandparent. When we were the parents, we were the ones in control, and we dealt with our extended family's issues. But, as grandparents, our relationship with our children and grandchildren is the only thing we can influence. When you can influence through peace and grace, it's a gift that serves everyone well.

You're modeling good behavior for your child and grandchildren by responding gracefully and courteously in every situation. Your example of kindness and respect may one day come back to you in surprising ways. So be patient, gracious, and kind to everyone involved—it's what's best for all concerned!

Pray

Dear Lord, thank you for our growing family.

While we are very excited about new babies and larger family gatherings, things sometimes go differently than planned when there are so many new people to factor in.

Let me be a peacemaker so that my child and their spouse can trust that, as far as I am able, I will do what's best for them and their family.

When there are moments of frustration, please remind me that you are in control and that those moments will pass. Knowing that you are with me and that your Spirit guides me with self-control and patience, I can get through anything.

Thank you for always providing exactly what I need to remain true to my faith.

In Jesus' name, I pray, amen.

15

WHAT HAPPENS AT NANA'S STAYS AT NANA'S

This is far more than a funny declaration intended to free grandparents of any responsibility for spoiling their grandchildren. Okay, it does function like that, but it's also more profound than that.

This is by far the most important mantra that we live by, whether the littles are at Nana and GranDan's or if they're at their great-grandma's house. As grandparents, our primary role is not to form and raise these little humans. That's their parents' job. Yes, we have a responsibility, when necessary, to provide backup as needed and to help these little ones act justly, love mercy, and walk humbly with God. Still, more importantly, they need us to give them a unique environment where they can rest and be free to do whatever they want.

You and your home are a reprieve from their usual routines. This becomes more apparent and important as the children grow older. They're bound by routines, rules, responsibilities, and consequences at home. At Nana's, there are no timelines, chores, or expectations. Disclaimer: it's not a free-for-all. But it's a different experience.

Snacks are unlimited; silliness is spurred on, and dance parties, squealing, and playing instruments are encouraged. Bedtime is determined by mood, not by the time on the clock. Breakfast might start with cookies and end with frozen waffles and eggs. Don't judge. Sometimes kids need to let loose and do things entirely outside the lines created at their own homes. Disclaimer: this only applies to sporadic visits. The rules are different if you are the primary caregiver for your grandchildren. Please don't say I didn't warn you!

> *Then my people will live in a peaceful settlement, In secure dwellings, and in undisturbed resting places;—Isaiah 32:18*

Being the fantastic mom she is, my daughter used to get upset if my granddaughters had two popsicles and a bowl of Doritos before bed at their great-grandma's house. She's mindful of proper nutrition, moderation of sweets, and consistency in her children's expectations. It was a (light-hearted) battle that neither side would win. Eventually, my daughter had the epiphany to remove herself from the equation and adopted the Vegas-style mantra. It freed her up to stop stressing about things out of her control and allowed those of us with the word grand in front of our titles to be the fun people we've been training to be for the past twenty-ish years.

The peace is commensurate with the fun, lack of proper nutrition, and dance parties. Being at grandma and grandpa's house also means a different kind of rest. For us, maybe it's one girl playing with a dollhouse, another girl building pyramids with red Solo Cups, and the other watching her favorite show. When they are allowed to do something on their own where they don't have to share or play nice together, it truly fills their buckets.

As a grandparent, you get the beautiful honor of being your grandchild's first best friend. This results from the trust you build with them by creating a fun, relaxing space in your home, providing gentle guidance, and providing teaching moments rather than proper discipline.

> *So then we pursue the things which make for peace and the building up of one another*
> —Romans 14:19

When your grandchildren are with you, follow their parents' discipline, but be more lenient than them. The children should have fun at your house and enjoy a different set of rules with you. That is not to say that they should get away with bad behavior, but recognize that not everything needs a consequence. Usually, a distraction is all that's required to make them forget the mischief.

It can be challenging for parents to take a step back and allow grandparents some freedom in this way. We love playing with them (and spoiling them rotten) and watching them grow into strong individuals. Communication between you and your children should be clear, open, and as positive as possible regarding expectations in your home.

As a GenXer, I've recognized that my Boomer/Silent parents were actively disciplining their grandchildren, correcting them, and engaging in parenting 2.0. My parents had fun moments, too, and they tried to create unique experiences for their grandchildren, but they saw themselves as a parenting extension of their children. Our generation also developed a discernment during our parenting years about whether certain things would seriously impact our children's personalities or well-being in the long term. We apply that to our grandchildren, too.

GenX was forced to be self-sufficient as children because we weren't "raised" or "parented." We figured out a lot on our own, and our minds were opened to different ways of viewing the world and parenting. I started out continuing my parents' method of grandparenting. After my daughter implemented WHNSN, that self-imposed pressure was lifted, and the freedom to have fun set in quickly.

Just as we provide a fun and energetic environment for our grandchildren, we also provide them with a gentle and slow pace when they need it. Their entire world can become so busy and rushed, and our house can be the respite they need. It's a space where they can do what they want, even if they only want to watch tv. TV isn't bad when the shows are appropriate and the watch time is limited. I don't know many people who don't get recharged by vegging in front of the tv for a bit so they can forget all the rules, responsibilities, and troubles that come with each day.

When we're offering our grandchildren their unique time with us, we are also providing our children time away from their kids, too. Even though your children love and trust you, they will still worry about their children when they're with you. Understanding WHNSN can help them relax, enjoy their kidless time, and remove any stress they might have about you not doing things "right."

Make sure your kids know that the rules are different at your house, but remember that if the entire family visits you, the parents still get to make the rules and the discipline choices. The best way to keep all the relationships healthy during these times is to make sure your grandchildren know that if mommy and daddy are present, they're the ones in charge. Undermining the parents—especially in front of the grandchildren—is an excellent way to spark an unnecessary argument.

We adore our time with our grandchildren and know they recognize the special relationship we've built with them. Since we have multiple grandchildren and multiple grandparent options nearby, sometimes one girl comes to our house, one girl goes to great-Grandma's house, and another stays home with mommy and daddy. They're afforded unique opportunities to dwell in peaceful places of safety and experience undisturbed rest. It's been one of the greatest gifts we can offer them.

On social media, I see funny videos from people who say their kids say that Nana's house is so awesome or they want to live with Nana because it's better there; they joke about how that woman is not the same one they grew up with. And we're not. We don't have to be parents and instill rules and responsibilities. We get to have fun, be spontaneous, and do everything the children want. That can't happen in their own home.

Grandparents play a unique role in the lives of their grandchildren. One that's different than their relationship with their parents. Grandparents are more likely to assume a mentor role for grandchildren. Grandparents may have more time on their hands than parents so they can spend more time with their grandchildren. Grandparents may be able to relate better to the children because of the opportunities we get to engage with them in more relaxed situations and through getting on the floor and playing with them.

> *and said, "Truly I say to you, unless you change and become like children, you will not enter the kingdom of heaven. So whoever will humble himself like this child, he is the greatest in the kingdom of heaven.—Matthew 18:3-4*

Because of this, we relate to our grandchildren differently than our children (or even our parents). We allow ourselves to be playful and silly. We allow ourselves to be seen in an entirely new light. If we let our guard down and become like those little children, we can be like them: people who are discovering things about themselves and the world around them, who have their hopes and dreams, and who deserve love no matter what happens in life! There's a different kind of renewal that comes with becoming a grandparent. It's like a do-over to figure out who we are and what we value. What a gift!

After all the rules have been broken, and routines are thrown out the window, your grandchildren return home and settle back into the safety of their routines and behavioral expectations.

The critical point to remember (perhaps share this with your adult children) is that we don't love our grandchildren more than our children; we get to enjoy a different relationship with them. They'll understand when it's their turn to institute the WHNSN rule.

When you have a close family—geographically and emotionally—we tend to communicate very openly. Parents often have conversations while forgetting little ears are listening and minds absorb every word they say. Sometimes those things will be shared with you. Children don't know what's private and what's not. They hear things, share them, and move on with their lives. Most times, it's not a big deal, but when they share something they probably shouldn't have, don't overreact.

If it's private but has no consequence of being shared with you, put it in the past and move on. However, if your grandchild shares information with you that they probably shouldn't share with anyone else or it's about a serious subject, then you should gently let your child know what was shared with you.

When these situations happen, share it without tones or looks of judgment—provide the information and leave it at that. No questions should be asked; you don't need to share personal opinions; just let them know what you know and change the subject. If they pursue the conversation further, that's their discretion.

This has happened to all of us as parents. Whether our kids told someone something embarrassing, deeply personal, or even exciting news that we weren't prepared to share, they almost always spilled the beans at some point. Do your kids a favor and don't overreact or judge or whatever you may be inclined to do. Unless the information comes from your adult child, it's not your business.

Pray

Lord, my time with my grandchildren is special to them and me. My relationship with my child and their spouse is unique and significant, so I always want to honor them as the final decision-makers for their children.

I pray, Lord, that you will help me be graceful and gentle when these concerns arise and that we will be able to agree that our home should be filled with fun and relaxed moments without emphasis on rules and responsibilities.

I love my family, Lord, and I am grateful for all the blessings you've provided through the love of my children and grandchildren.

In Jesus' Holy name, I pray, amen.

16

NATURE & NURTURE

As your grandchildren grow, watching their personalities develop, their talents revealed, and other little traits that will surprise you will be beautiful. They'll become the mini-me of one of their parents, or they might even be a miniature version of you! The beauty of grandchildren is the same as children in that they are a perfect little combination of their parents with a sprinkle of something unique to them.

Birth order also affects their personality traits in unique ways. My daughter is an only child and therefore has the attributes of a first child. Rest assured, she does not have only child syndrome. She has some aspects of only-child status, but more so, her first-child traits are strong, and I'm grateful for that.

Seeing my grandchildren's various personalities based on birth order has been so fun. My daughter has three girls, and their birth order traits are almost quintessential.

I encourage you to explore birth order as your children's families grow. It is an incredible phenomenon. My oldest granddaughter, Eliza, is a leader. She's bold and brave and an excellent communicator. She's protective of her sisters and parents and is a motivated learner with a competitive spirit.

My middle granddaughter, Evelynn, is a firecracker. She's funny, and fun-loving; she's imaginative, brave, and strong. She's a follower and doesn't have a competitive bone in her body. She's sweet, sensitive, and stubborn.

My youngest granddaughter, Everley, is an empath. An old soul who keeps a finger on the pulse of a room and follows the rules. She's a peacemaker and thoughtful beyond comprehension.

Eliza is an early riser who loves to embrace the day with an eager spirit. Evelynn sleeps late and needs time to get into the day's groove. Everley can wake early, be excited to see the sun, or sleep in a little; there's no difference in her demeanor. The different natures of the three girls are only a small example of how they are different.

Apart from their birth order traits, your grandbabies will have unique natures about them that are worthy of identifying and nurturing. Birth order traits and individual character become more fascinating as a grandparent because we have more time and availability to notice these things.

When we were parenting and raising our children, life was moving at epic speeds, and we couldn't keep up. There was school, activities, meltdowns, and discipline, and we didn't have the chance to soak up who our children were. Just me?

This may be why grandparenting is so special. It allows us to connect with the offspring of our offspring in ways we never could during our parenting years. We are blessed to be more in tune and attentive to all the things that make them unique.

One way to more intentionally engage with your grandchildren is to have dates with them. First and foremost, encourage their parents to have one-on-one mommy and daddy dates because this is a game changer in many ways. But as a grandparent, your dates with them are essential, too. When you take them out to lunch, the donut shop, or the park, it's a different emotional experience and connection than when they're at your house for a visit or sleepover. Dates with the littles build up beautiful moments that grow and evolve your relationship with them. Five stars, highly recommend.

> *"And He is the radiance of His glory and the exact representation of His nature, and upholds all things by the word of His power. When He had made purification of sins, He sat down at the right hand of the Majesty on high,—Hebrews 1:3*

One of the most beneficial aspects of getting to know your grandchildren from these perspectives is how it opens your mind to the issues children today face. It will equip you to help your children navigate the eventual parenting difficulties so that consideration is given to each child's traits and nature.

When you are close to your grandchildren, you can help nurture them through activities and using examples based on their natural interests and abilities. You might surprise yourself by realizing you enjoy the same things that interest them. We gave our youngest granddaughter a pottery wheel for Christmas. She wanted me to teach her how to use it and help her make her first flower pot. By the time we were done, I was so inspired and wanted a pottery wheel for myself! I had no idea I would enjoy something like that so much.

You can bring out your grandchildren's natural talents by helping them engage in activities congruent with their nature.

Begin by encouraging exploration. Suggest various activities or lessons so they can figure out their interests. This will help them develop a sense of self-awareness and discover their talents and passions.

Create opportunities for growth once they've chosen an activity. Provide opportunities for your grandchildren to practice their skills and learn new ones. This could include teaching them game rules, practicing with them in the yard, or providing materials and space to experiment and create.

Offer support and encouragement so they know they can share both their excitement and frustrations. Show interest in what your grandchild is doing and offer words of encouragement. This will help them feel confident in their abilities and motivated to continue exploring.

It takes time for children to develop their talents and skills. If you have high-achievers, help them focus on the journey and the progress made along the way instead of focusing on the success that comes with mastery.

Understanding what motivates a child has an impact on how we nurture their growth, how we guide them, and how we communicate with them. Getting to know your grandchildren on a deeper level means you'll be able to help them and help their parents in valuable ways. Rather than speaking from general experiences, you'll be able to conscientiously create experiences and solutions that connect with your grandchildren in a meaningful way.

Part of this nurturing applies to helping them navigate their feelings. Children go through confusing or upsetting moments, and we can guide them through exploring their thoughts and feelings.

One of my granddaughters enjoys a genuine give-and-take in conversations when working through challenging situations. That said, she will often wait until someone else pursues the conversation. Still, once she's willing to talk, it's a two-way conversation that leads to better understanding and typically resolving the problem. Another one of the girls operates better when given the time and space to reflect on her feelings. If you ask her to talk, she clams up tight. But she'll share when the pressure is off and you let her settle into a safe space of reflection. The other, well, she dives right into conflict and resolution. When upset, she immediately brings it to light and moves on.

I can't stress enough the amazement I feel when witnessing the unique ways these girls navigate life. It's such an exciting time, and because we're GenX, we experience it more up close and personally. I adore the relationships I have with my grandchildren.

> *and let's consider how to encourage one another in love and good deeds,*—Hebrews 10:24

A friend shared with me that she sometimes wondered if one of her grandchildren would irritate her. It's possible. Difficult children need nurturing according to their nature. As we hopefully learned during our parenting years, our more challenging children fare better when we lean into their tendencies rather than push back against them. Creativity is vital not only in parenting but also in grandparenting.

When your grandchild's nature includes undesirable behaviors or traits, this can come with overwhelming guilt for any negative feelings you might have toward them. You could limit your time with that particular child while getting to know and understand their personality. Study their parents' methods of interacting with them and figure out how you can put your spin on that.

The most important thing to remember is that this is a child of God, and he created them perfectly in His image. It might not seem like it when you're grasping for sanity. This scripture is a profound reminder that God started something within them, and you'll see God's plan as they grow. You'll need to have a little patience and a lot of creativity along the way.

In the meantime, you can use scripture to help you guide your challenging little one. Nurturing a child with the word of the Lord is a beautiful experience. I can't imagine a better way to instruct, lead, and love your grandchildren than through the grace of our Heavenly Father.

> *These words, which I am commanding you today, shall be on your heart. And you shall repeat them diligently to your sons and speak of them when you sit in your house, when you walk on the road, when you lie down, and when you get up.* —*Deuteronomy 6:6-7*

When you have a visit coming up with your grandchild, review a couple of scriptures that you can share with them to help them focus and feel the love that you have for them, as well as the love that God has for them. The scripture you choose should have a focus that will resonate with the child and be at a level of understanding appropriate for their age.

This part on nurturing is heavy in scripture. This is intentional so that you can see God has something to say about everything. There is nothing new under the sun. As a grandparent who cares about creating a positive relationship with your grandchildren, it's essential that you know how to apply God's word to nurturing your grandchildren. Whether you encourage them to grow in their natural gifts or navigate some annoyances that need special handling, God's got you.

> *All your sons will be taught by the Lord; And the well-being of your sons will be great.*
> —*Isaiah 54:13*

This final scripture brings me so much joy. If we allow our grandchildren to be taught by the Lord (guiding with scripture), He promises they will experience great peace. In a world with so much conflict, God's promise of peace for His children brings comfort that can be found nowhere else.

Pray

Dear God, I'm so excited to get to know my grandchildren! Getting to know each little personality as they come along and watching them grow is a blessing!

Thank you for bringing these babies to our family and for the opportunities I have to impact them in meaningful ways.

Lord, you are the Creator of everything and have created every person for a purpose. You have given my grandchildren unique gifts, attributes, and talents, and I can't wait to witness how you've blessed them.

In Jesus' Name, I pray, amen.

17

SPOIL THE CHILD

This season of life generally leads us to a more significant focus on self-reflection. We're in our "mid-life" years, and everything is changing. And as we chart this new course, it can hit hard to realize we are in a season of high impact with our adult children.

How we raised them may be translated into how they raise their children. We'll see the best of our efforts repeated and brought back to life, and we'll also never see the worst of our parenting moments, praise God.

To see our children emulate us and hold on to pieces of their childhood that were most impactful to them is honestly one of the most rewarding aspects of parenting. Unfortunately, we don't get to experience it until they're adults! When it happens, though, it's heartwarming and gives us a sense of humility to know that we did something worth repeating to another generation.

I think it's part of the reason we can so easily separate ourselves from the discipline and "raising" of our grandchildren. When we were given the crown of grandchildren, we were given a gift to enjoy a quiet spirit and the favor we receive from our Heavenly Father, who teaches us precisely what we need to know in every season.

Our children's discipline methods won't be precisely the same as ours, even if they emulate some of our methods. Not the same as how we were disciplined by our parents nor the way we disciplined our children. They'll do it better than us.

As you watch them, you will learn more than you teach and you will become a student of child-raising by watching your children raise their children. When you thought you'd spend this time imparting all your wisdom, you find out your kids are more creative and intelligent than you.

A new generation deserves fresh thinking and mindful intentionality instead of repeating what we know. Because our parents did something or we did something does not mean it was the proper method.

Each generation learns something new about "training up a child in the way they should go," In many ways, it's so much better than generations before. Children are bright and understand more than our generation and previous generations we give them credit for. It doesn't take dropping the hammer on them to get them to learn the lesson at hand. I can't help but wish that I had been as aware of this as a parent.

My daughter and son-in-law have found a gentle way of disciplining over the years. There's been a lot of trial and error, and they have mastered their methodology. That doesn't mean they never have new issues, but that they apply the same approach, which is gentle and spirit-driven.

When I've been asked for my take on specific behavioral issues, I try to steer them in a direction that I know is consistent with their approach to discipline and guidance. I think the one thing I've turned to more than anything is asking the time question I've mentioned before. Will this matter next week, next month, or next year? If it will matter beyond the next month, then it's worth fretting over, but if the issue isn't going to turn into a personality or respect problem, then it's best not to dwell on the little things. Depending on the situation, these timeframe questions can help them appropriately craft their responses to defiance.

We know that defiance in children starts earlier than we anticipate and is the beginning of independence. When we understand their nature, we can better guide our littles through their defiance to help them learn rather than fail.

It's easier for me to see it that way and understand the truth because I've already raised my child. I'm on the other side, and I've seen that everything turns out just fine. When you're in the throes of parenting, it can feel like every little thing must be given attention so that the child turns out to be a good human.

Unfortunately, it's hard to relax and believe things will be okay in the middle of it.

As a grandparent, you can help the most by providing calm during the storm of difficult parenting seasons. Assure them they're doing great even if they've made a not-so-great choice for discipline (aside from abuse). We've all made mistakes as parents, and the shame and guilt stick with us. We don't need to remind other parents of these moments.

This is especially true if your child attempts to break generational discipline issues. Your support is vital for them to turn the tide.

You have also given me the shield of Your salvation, And Your right hand upholds me; And Your gentleness makes me great.—Psalm 18:35

This scripture is so beautiful it stirs up deep emotions in me. I've messed up so much in my life, and God still gave me the shield of salvation, His hand has been at my back, supporting me in everything I do, and indeed His gentleness *has* made me great. I know I'm only great in His eyes because He made me and knows me at my core. He makes everything great.

As a grandparent, when I reflect on these words, it resonates within me that grandparenting is a lot like this. We are the consistent hand of support, and our gentleness toward our grandchildren can lead them to great things. As you approach all things having to do with discipline and guidance, remember that everything done with gentleness and a supportive hand is how we respond like Jesus.

As I've covered discipline methods, the most important thing to remember is that discipline is a parenting issue, and you are not the parent. If conversations with your children provide an opening for you to provide positive input, that's acceptable. Otherwise, take time to discern whether the issue is important enough to bring up.

The one caveat is if the children exhibit behaviors that require further addressing or consequences. In the first several years, when the girls were with us, I'd report the behavioral issues, and the problems would be dealt with at home. Eventually, we realized that wasn't working for us and our relationship with our grandchildren, nor for the parents to deal with issues once they got home.

My daughter realized she didn't want us to have to be disciplinarians. She wanted us to enjoy our time with the girls, setting aside the usual discipline expectations, which allowed us to relax more. Unless something is so egregious that it requires parental involvement, we handle learning moments quickly, move on, and forget them. Besides, when children aren't at home, they typically don't have the same discipline needs.

This is one of the many reasons you and your grandchildren will have such a special relationship, especially while they're little. Parents can't (or shouldn't) be friends with their children until they're adults. There needs to be a clear boundary for the parent/child relationship.

Discipline is not the responsibility of a grandparent. The parent's job is to discipline their child correctly so they grow up with healthy morals and values. Many parents attempt to evade this responsibility by passing it off to others, including grandparents. This can harm the child's development and cause them to have a skewed sense of morality and responsibility towards others. If your grandchildren's parents ask you to provide discipline when they misbehave, remind them that disciplining children is one of their most important responsibilities.

If they insist you do it, explain your position outside your grandchildren's presence, and stand firm in that decision. This is also a good time for you to provide gentle suggestions for your child to handle your grandchildren's behavior so that you don't have to.

> *For whom the Lord loves He disciplines, Just as a father disciplines the son in whom he delights.—Proverbs 3:12*

If all else fails, remember that there are other ways that you can instill values in your grandchild while still allowing their parents to do the bulk of disciplining themselves. So long as your grandchild learns responsibility, morals, and values, that is all that matters in the end.

Some people view grandparenting as a do-over for parenting their children. Wouldn't we all enjoy parenting our children again knowing what we know now? I imagine our parents would, too. But grandparenting has nothing to do with parenting. The word is meant to define the relationship or lineage of the family members; however, this is a season of reinventing yourself or returning to yourself. Who you were before you became a parent.

There are seven, eight, and nine years' differences in age between my three siblings and me. I became an aunt at the age of eleven. I was young and fabulous and much more chill than my siblings, who became parents while I was a child. As I entered my teen years with nieces who were toddlers, I had plenty of thoughts and comments about child-rearing. I remember my sister saying, "I can't wait until you become a mom and your kid is perfect." She was being sarcastic, of course, and she was right. As an aunt, I wasn't responsible for how my nieces and nephews turned out. I felt responsible for their safety and happiness but not for their upbringing to ensure they became good humans. I didn't know enough to think that deeply.

My siblings are all Boomers. I'm the only GenXer of my parents' kids. They parented their children primarily the way our parents raised them. My sister had more GenX parenting tendencies, but my brother was all Boomer. My upbringing is drastically different, even though we're from the same family.

I think of parenting as being an architect. You created and raised your children in that role as though you were designing a museum. You developed their lives through education, activities, values, and family ties. There are generations of influence within them. You guided them until you recognized your work was good, and they were ready for their purpose.

Your grandchildren are your leisurely walk through the Museum after it's open to the public. Your grandchildren are the artifacts, the masterful paintings, the bits of history you get to revisit, and the glimpse of an exciting future for your family. This is your time to study them, enjoy them, share moments with them and create a legacy for them that will become part of *their* history.

Your grandparenting role is not a do-over of your parenting season. When you receive that crown, it's a crown of freedom. Freedom to nurture and love your children's children. Freedom to be who you are outside of the stress and responsibility of parenting.

Pray

Lord, I am so grateful to be blessed with children and grandchildren. Through your grace, I got through those parenting years, and my children are so wonderful, and I'm so proud you chose me for them.

Now that I'm a grandparent, it should be different, and my time with them should be fun and filled with moments that make great memories for them.

I will always be there whenever my child needs my help, and I'm thankful our relationship includes open and honest communication.

Lord, bless my grandchildren and me as we learn and grow together. In the name of your son, Jesus, I pray, amen.

18

YOU ARE A CHILD OF GOD

We can get so caught up in life that we can fall into the trap of deriving our identity as a parent/daughter/spouse, etc. Your identity in Christ is the truth of who you are that influences those relationships. Somewhere along the way, becoming a grandparent has become one of *the most* defining moments we can experience. There is so much promise and hope in a new generation.

Who has God called you to be concerning these little children?

> *You will make known to me the way of life; In Your presence is fullness of joy; In Your right hand there are pleasures forever.*—Psalm 16:11

Joy is found first in the Lord.

Because we love our children so much, we're deeply involved in their lives. Everything we do is to protect them, love them, and pray that everyone they come into contact with will do the same. Often, parents become so immersed in their children that their identity is found in them. Be it vicariously living through their athletic pursuits, obsessing over their ease with academics, or wanting so badly to be their best friends, and some parents are consumed by who they are in their children's eyes.

This is unhealthy for the parent/child relationship and not beneficial for grandparent/grandchild relationships.

As followers of Jesus, our identity must be found in Him first, foremost, and always. When we ingrain our identity in Christ, everything else falls into place.

Resting in the truth of who we are in God gives us the freedom to be who we are to God, ourselves, and our family. The energy you spend trying to be all things to all people to be liked—even in your own family—is a treadmill that never slows down.

Nurturing yourself and getting to know who you are in Christ, uncovering your identity as a child of God, is the start of building the most important legacy you can leave your grandchildren. It may be part of your plan when you die to leave your children and grandchildren money, jewelry, and precious mementos for them to remember you by, but the only inheritance that matters is eternal life.

As you deepen your identity in Christ and live that out each day in front of your children and grandchildren, you create a beautiful example for your family. It's always possible to pursue the life you've always wanted. Consistently seeking peace and deepening your faith shows that you value your relationships, beginning with God.

Many of us are raised in the church, fall away from the church when we go to college, and seek God again when we start a family. This doesn't apply to everyone, but it happens a lot. Being apart from family, being influenced by new friends from different cultures and religions, and having the desire to belong are all drivers of this falling away.

Even if you are starting to feel drawn back to Jesus, your family can see that it's never too late to pursue a beautiful life rooted in faith.

Leaving a legacy can and should be more than material in nature. A legacy of love, kindness, and faith has a much more significant impact than any amount of money.

> *Your words were found and I ate them, And Your words became a joy to me and the delight of my heart; For I have been called by Your name, Lord God of armies.*
> —Jeremiah 15:16

The words of the Lord are spiritual nourishment. When consume them, it becomes effortless to find our identity in God. Knowing the bible has something to say about everything we will encounter or endure in our lives is comforting. It helps us to feel seen and understood. Jesus knew our trials left us words of sustenance.

When God calls me Home, I want them to reflect on this aspect of me. But more importantly, I want them to forever reflect on my love for them and how I was centered on Jesus Christ. I want them to think of me anytime they face difficulty and remember how I encouraged them to pray through everything and trust God.

When they think of me, I want it to be impossible for them not to also think of Jesus. I'm not perfect in my attempts to achieve this, but it's always top of mind to keep me focused on God.

When you place your identity in God, everything else falls into place. You are no longer defined by your mistakes or circumstances but by His unending love for you. When you know who you are in Christ, you can face anything life throws your way.

Looking back on Jeremiah 15:16, we can see that when we consume God's word, that becomes the delight of our hearts, and we truly recognize that we are called according to God's name.

What does this mean? In short, Jeremiah was referring to his anguish of being somewhat of an outcast and alone because of his faith. He found the fullness of life in the word of God, which is the bread we survive on. He ate, or consumed, the word which brought him joy and a calling from the Lord.

There is no greater peace than knowing that you are fully known and loved by the Creator of the universe. So if you're feeling lost or struggling to find your way, know that you can always find your identity in God. He will never leave or forsake you, and He will help you through whatever challenges come your way. Trust in Him, and let Him lead you to the abundant life He has waiting for you.

In short, when you place your identity in God, you find the freedom that comes with no longer being defined by your mistakes or circumstances. You can pursue a life of purpose and meaning as you walk with the Lord. If you ever feel like everything is falling apart, remember that God loves and knows you perfectly—and nothing will ever change His love for you. The peace, joy, and contentment that come from knowing who He created you to be are more significant than any earthly trial or struggle could ever offer. Place your trust in Him today—your eternal identity is waiting for you!

> *Now flee from youthful lusts and pursue righteousness, faith, love, and peace with those who call on the Lord from a pure heart.—2 Timothy 2:22*

GenX has a strong sense of self-identity in our strength, resilience, and independence. We don't need help with anything, we don't want to talk about our feelings, and we don't dwell on failures - at least externally. We can tend to beat ourselves up internally, but we don't reveal that to others.

This makes us some of the most rigid shells to break when it comes to letting our guard down and being vulnerable, especially in areas of faith.

As we mature, I think we're beginning to recognize the struggle of where we fit in and who we want to be as we enter new life seasons. As for me, I always expected I would be more settled in who I am by the time I reached fifty. The truth is, I'm still learning so much about myself primarily because of my openness to allowing God to speak to me through the Holy Spirit and being more attentive to my needs and values.

When we struggle with understanding who we are because of our life experiences, we create unrest and confusion for those around us. I believe the only way to make peace with ourselves finally is to find our identity in Christ.

We were made in His image. To be that which is good, to share love, and to help others. It may seem oversimplified, but it's truly why we're here.

Many people struggle to find their sense of self, searching for happiness and fulfillment as they try to navigate the ups and downs of life. Sometimes, that identity is found in harmful, earthly idols. But when we place our identity in God, who knows us perfectly and loves us completely, we find peace and contentment that nothing on this earth can offer.

> *Blessed be the God and Father of our Lord Jesus Christ, who has blessed us with every spiritual blessing in the heavenly places in Christ, just as He chose us in Him before the foundation of the world, that we would be holy and blameless before Him. In love He predestined us to adoption as sons and daughters through Jesus Christ to Himself, according to the good pleasure of His will, to the praise of the glory of His grace, with which He favored us in the Beloved.—Ephesians 1:3-6*

I've seen one consistency among GenX: a tendency to pursue faith later in life. Perhaps we were raised in the church, then we went away from it for a time, and then eventually, marriage and children brought us back to it.

In our grandparenting years, we seem to especially pursue faith not only because we understand the importance of cultivating our relationship with Jesus while we influence our grandchildren for God, but also because we're getting older. And with age comes awareness of our mortality, and with mortality comes eternity.

I choose eternity with Jesus. You can, too, if you haven't already. After enduring life on this earth, I can guarantee you I'm not taking any chances on where I'm spending my life after death. I want paradise. I want easy living. I want pure, unfathomable joy.

So many benefits - besides the obvious - come from pursuing life with God.

For one thing, when you know your worth is found in a loving relationship with God, it allows you to stop using earthly pursuits like material wealth, status, or achievements to define yourself. Instead, your focus shifts outward—toward helping others discover the same joy that comes from knowing Christ. You can share the good news about God's unconditional love without feeling like you have anything else to prove or protect.

You can also shift why you want to achieve specific life goals. Until now, maybe you were seeking your parents' approval or wanted a way to make a good living and support your family. When you understand that you are a child of God, your focus shifts to glorifying Him, furthering His kingdom through how you conduct yourself and treat others, and being the person He made you to be.

Knowing who you are in Jesus changes your relationships with your family and others. The deepening of connection allows you to feel safe, valued, and qualified to share His deep, unconditional love with others.

When we're not around fellow Jesus followers, it's easy to forget that we are already children of God. We're already precious to Him, He loves us and wants us with Him in eternity. He's extended an invitation and patiently waits for you to accept.

> *"And I will be a father to you, And you shall be sons and daughters to Me," Says the Lord Almighty.* —2 Corinthians 6:18

He's not going to force Himself into your life. You've had a lifelong invitation with no RSVP date. You can accept it anytime. You'll never be turned away at the gates of the party.

If you're feeling lost or struggling to find your place in this world, know that placing your identity in God can help lead you toward the abundant life He has planned for you. Turn to Him with all your doubts and fears—and let Him begin transforming every area of your heart and mind today!

Pray

Father, your Word is proof that I am yours. Father, let your Holy Spirit wash over me as I seek your peace. I can feel and hear your presence during times of true stillness.

Father, God, though I fall away from time to time, I know that you sent Jesus as my Savior. I trust that you love me no matter my circumstances or season of life. I am so grateful for your grace and mercy.

Guide me, Lord, to follow you and seek your instruction for my life. I know you see me for who you made me to be. Please help me to fulfill that purpose.

I pray in the name of my Lord and Savior, Jesus Christ, amen.

19

YOUR FUTURE IS NOW

I didn't think much about my middle life or later years . . . even retirement, until my first grandchild came along. She filled my soul with a desire to do something different, to live a more meaningful life and do more meaningful work.

My daughter had a similar effect on me when I became a mom. It was a different type of motivation. Being a mom made me more driven to be successful, earn money and support my daughter to give her a great life. It was about responsibility and provision.

As a grandparent, the motivation was to figure out how to be more available for my grandchildren, avoid living to work and create a legacy that made a difference and made my family proud.

I've always been creative, with writing as my primary art, and I also seemed to be the "good idea" person, so I used that to create a business that would pave the way for me to do so much more than I ever imagined. Most importantly, my venture into entrepreneurship provided the life I craved to have a flexible schedule and be available to my family.

It is no accident that I quit my corporate job in July of 2015, and the next month, I launched my business, and a week later, I learned that my Dad had lung cancer that metastasized to the brain. I put the brakes on my business and focused on my parents.

God had His hand in every aspect of the entrepreneurial journey because He knew what was coming. By His grace, I could be with my Mom and Dad at every one of his appointments, treatments, and hospitalizations. I was blessed to be able to spend every day of what turned out to be eleven weeks left of his life.

If I had still been working in my corporate job, there is no way I could have been there for him. I'd have been doing unimportant work, missing the final weeks and days of my Dad's time with us.

After my dad passed, I spent time mourning, and eventually, I could hear his voice telling me enough is enough; it's time to get back to work. I jumped with both feet into my business again, a gift company using products made by small businesses to create beautiful and meaningful gift boxes.

Eliza, our first grandchild, was four years old when I started my business. Initially, she loved to play with the packaging and ask questions about the products. By age five, she began to inquire more about the company, how it works, and how I make money. I explained everything to her and shared that part of my business model included giving back. There were several nonprofit organizations that we believe in that we chose to provide a portion of our profits to. That excited her, and she wanted to help.

She started by simply helping to put products on shelves or fill boxes with crinkle paper so I could prepare the gifts. Over the years, her interest and involvement grew so she could assemble all the packaging and arrange the gift boxes from start to finish. She loved to see how high she could stack the orders before I'd speak up for fear they'd fall over. The fun we had and the moments we shared created a connection between us and developed an entrepreneurial spirit within her.

In perfect timing, a Children's Business Fair was launched in our city.

I took my granddaughters to the first one to see what it was all about. We walked the aisles enjoying the creativity of these business-minded youth, and Eliza knew she wanted to start her own business, and she wanted it to be like mine, where she also gave back.

By the time the following business fair came along, Eliza had created her business making throw-style pillows with positive messages (You Are Loved, You Are Brave, You Are Kind, etc.) written on tags that were sewn onto them.

For every pillow she sells, she gives one to a child in foster care. She spent time with her great-grandma (my mom), learning how to sew and stuff and finishing the pillows. She's participated in the business fair every year since, and she gets better at sewing and understanding the process each year. She can make the pillows from start to finish with my mom's oversight. What a blessing this bonding time has been for the two of them!

Again, had I stayed in my corporate job, there would have been no opportunity for me to pour into Eliza and allow her to recognize her gifts, interests, and talents.

I now have a different business that I run. Still, Eliza works on her pillow business, continuing to grow it in unique and insightful ways.

From creating a career out of necessity to take care of my family to building a business on my God-given gifts has changed my life. I have margin and flexibility, I have control over my income, and I can make a difference in the lives of my family members simply because I can be there for them.

> *Therefore, my beloved brothers and sisters, be firm, immovable, always excelling in the work of the Lord, knowing that your labor is not in vain in the Lord.*
> *—1 Corinthians 15:58*

You are creative in some way. You have a passion that can be spun into a business opportunity. You have the ability and the means to create a life in this crowning season that will offer contentment, satisfaction, and a legacy unique to you and your family.

Even if you don't need to work or generate income, your gifts can be used to bless others. My aunt loves doing diamond dot art projects. I'd be willing to say she's obsessed with them. She has made so many that she's gotten to the point that she's fast at them and takes creative liberty with them. If the design is created with color in a particular area that she doesn't like, or if she thinks it'll be enhanced with a different color, she changes it and adds her creative touch. I'm sure you're thinking the obvious: How many diamond art projects can one person hang on their walls?

She might have a few that adorn her own space, and others have become gifts, but the overwhelming majority of her creations are being used to bless others. She now sells her diamond art projects at farmer's markets and craft fairs and donates the money to her church. She loves to create and found that if she sells art projects for donation purposes, she can do what she enjoys without building a backyard shed to store them.

Maybe you have a love for gardening. Children love learning about gardening and watching those planted seeds turn into little sprouts they eventually harvest for dinner. It's a beautiful way to build confidence and excitement in a little one. Take it further and donate some overgrowth to your elderly neighbors with your grandchildren by your side. Show them what it means to love your neighbor. Perhaps you can do some canning and sell some of your creations at a farmer's market.

I know you have a unique gift that is a blessing to others. Whether you want to start a business or do something else that brings you joy, I encourage you to pursue these things. Share them. Not just *what* you're doing but share *why* you're doing it. Give your family and friends a deep dive into that memory that sits so vividly in your mind of the time you realized you'd love to own a catering company because of that time you prepared the entire menu for your mom's 60th birthday party.

But you already had a job, being a caterer was a distant dream, and you had no idea how to start and run a business, so you're still running the eight to five treadmill in an office. Imagine the fun you'd have baking up your custom creations with your grandchildren helping you in the kitchen!

Maybe at some point in time, you said, "one day," I'm going to be a caterer, or I'd like to get into real estate when the kids are older. If you're reading this, your kids have kids. Now is your time to be true to yourself.

It is always possible to start something new. We weren't meant to do only one thing in life when it comes to working. We are made to learn and grow within our knowledge and creativity. What we did straight out of high school or college isn't necessarily what we're meant to do now. When given a chance to speak with young people who aren't sure what they want to do in life, I encourage them to think about what they want to do for the next ten years.

So much pressure is placed on knowing who we want to be when we grow up, getting a degree in that, and working in that one field until we retire. That's a lot of pressure to know what you want to do for your entire life.

This applies now, too. It's the perfect time to reimagine your future because you have decades ahead of you. Work in your gifts!

Please keep this message from being lost on you. You were made for more. You were given a gift by the actual Creator, whose creativity is unmatched. He placed a little spark inside you for something of His design. What would the wildfire look like if you breathed life into that spark?

Let's say you're a fantastic violinist. You've been playing since you were a kid and loved it. But how can you use that talent to make money? "I could teach violin," you say. And sure, that's one way to go about it. But there are other options as well. You could play at fine restaurants or special events. You could start a YouTube channel where you teach videos on how to play different songs on your violin, or you could sell your music on streaming channels.

Mentally divide your passions into two categories: things you enjoy and skills you've acquired. Your skills, talents, and interests are more marketable than you think. There's a good chance you already have a built-in fanbase that would like to see what else you can do.

It's never too late or too soon to start a business. I genuinely believe that this season of mid-life was made for reinventing ourselves. We're finally more in tune with who we are at our core, we know what we value in life, and we are likely ready to do things a little differently or create more margin to give us time to do what we enjoy, like spending time with our grandchildren.

This might be difficult for you to consider because we were raised by Boomers who loyally served one company their entire working life, and you might be doing the same thing. Leaving your current position or company might seem stressful to venture into the unknown. There's much to consider, like insurance benefits, a reliable salary, and retirement.

One thing I know for sure is that we get one life. Let's make sure we're happy, not just existing.

GenX created a generation filled with people who are creative, inspiring, and not afraid of work. Your impact on your children helped them see their value and inspired them to try new things. As a grandparent, you can grow that role into one of the nontraditional activities with your grandchildren, like helping them start a business, nurturing their natural talents, and building up their confidence in their abilities.

If you explore entrepreneurship, you could be in that sweet spot of working remotely, which means you can travel whenever you want and take your work with you. Work no longer takes eight to ten hours in an office to accomplish. It's much easier to be more focused and productive when you work from home, which translates into shorter workdays and more time to enjoy life.

If you're close to retirement and plan to finish your career, start considering what your retirement looks like. Are you going to remain unemployed? Will you consider entrepreneurship? What do you want to spend your time, energy, and retirement funds on? You have so many active and fulfilling years ahead of you. It would be best to find out what your *life* holds once your children are grown and have their own families.

Your grandchildren grow up, too, and you need to have your own thing so that you aren't lost when reality strikes. Set up your camp, and your children and grandchildren will always know where to find you.

> 'For I know the plans that I have for you,' declares the Lord, 'plans for prosperity and not for disaster, to give you a future and a hope.'—Jeremiah 29:11

We might be "midlife," but we still have a future! God has declared a future over us that comes with hope.

Your crown comes with freedom in all things, including reinventing your life and livelihood. Whatever it means for you, go forward in God, knowing that He has created this life for you to experience in a way only God can do.

Pray

Heavenly Father, you created me with talents and dreams that I still need to explore fully. You instilled in me a desire to serve through volunteering my time, but I've never set aside that time.

Lord, I pray for your guidance as I consider how I can apply my gifts to a new career or volunteering. Please reveal your plans and lead me to where I can make the most impact. I'm open to doing something new, but I need to figure out where to begin. I'm ready to hear from you and place my focus where I can do the most good while making myself more available for my family.

I pray this in the name of Jesus, amen.

20

FRUITS OF THE SPIRIT

The Fruits of the Holy Spirit are the natural aspects of our being that God planted within us that we rely on the Holy Spirit to bring out, but life and worldliness cause us to forget our default settings.

God intended and desired us to respond to all people and concerns with the fruits He planted, but those people and problems turn us into worrisome beings who fear the wrong things. We are only to fear God. God did not plant roots of fear or anger, or offense in us. We learned these things from this world. Those things are the rotted waste of worldly fruits.

When we look at a fruit tree or a vineyard, we see that there are two types of fruit: good and bad. Good fruit comes from healthy trees and vines, while bad fruit comes from unhealthy ones. So when it comes to our lives as Christians, there are also two types of fruit: good and bad. Good fruits come from healthy relationships, while bad fruits come from unhealthy relationships with others (or no relationship with anyone at all).

As we follow the example of God's love, we can take heart that not only is love the answer to all aspects of life and people, all of the fruits of the Holy Spirit apply to everything we may encounter as grandparents. As I researched scripture for this book, almost all of them have something to do with at least one of the Fruits of the Spirit. They are integral to everyday living and should not be dismissed as a list of words. They are the same characteristics by which we must live to not only live a peaceful life but also bear witness to the Holy Spirit's work.

Living out the fruits of the Holy Spirit in our grandparenting can positively impact our relationship with our adult children.

The Fruits of the Holy Spirit are Love, Joy, Peace, Patience, Kindness, Goodness, Faithfulness, Gentleness, and Self-control.

The fruits of the holy spirit are essential because they help us become more like Christ and experience His love in our lives. When we live out these characteristics, life is better and more fulfilling.

Let's explore each fruit in a little more depth.

Love

> *"This is My commandment, that you love one another, just as I have loved you."*
> *—John 15:12*
>
> *Above all, keep fervent in your love for one another, because love covers a multitude of sins.—1 Peter 4:8*

Do we need any better explanation of love? God is love. God made us in His image. We love because He loves.

Loving others is the reason we can forgive. It's why we can exist in harmony in a world filled with people who are so different from us. Love allows us to be vulnerable and open to others. It would be impossible to experience any other emotion or fruit of the Spirit if we didn't first have love.

Joy

> and though you have not seen Him, you love Him, and though you do not see Him now, but believe in Him, you greatly rejoice with joy inexpressible and full of glory, obtaining as the outcome of your faith, the salvation of your souls.—1 Peter 1:8-9
>
> Boast in His holy name; Let the heart of those who seek the Lord be joyful.
> —1 Chronicles 16:10

Joy is born from love.

When we are joyful despite our circumstances, we can encourage others through this and may even inspire them to seek God, too.

When you have the joy of the Holy Spirit in your life, it can be contagious. Your grandchildren will see the joy in your eyes and your smile, and they will want to know what makes you so happy.

You can tell them it is because you have God's love in your heart. You can explain to them how when you pray and ask God for His help, He gives you the strength to overcome any hurdle. And finally, you can let them know that you have the joy of the Holy Spirit because it is a gift from God.

Peace

> And the peace of God, which surpasses all comprehension, will guard your hearts and minds in Christ Jesus.—Philippians 4:7
>
> May mercy, peace, and love be multiplied to you.—Jude 1:2

This peace is unlike the world's peace based on circumstances. The world's peace is fleeting and often dependent on things beyond our control. The peace of the Holy Spirit is a deep and lasting peace that comes from God Himself. It is a peace that transcends all understanding.

Grandparents, let us strive to live lives that are full of the peace of the Holy Spirit. As we do, we will be able to impart this peace to our grandchildren, equipping them to handle whatever life throws their way.

Patience

> *Yet for this reason I found mercy, so that in me as the foremost sinner Jesus Christ might demonstrate His perfect patience as an example for those who would believe in Him for eternal life.—1 Timothy 1:16*

> *preach the word; be ready in season and out of season; correct, rebuke, and exhort, with great patience and instruction.—2 Timothy 4:2*

As a grandparent, you have the unique opportunity to impact the next generation significantly. You can share your wisdom and experience with your grandchildren and help them to grow in their faith. One of the most important things you can do is to model patience.

You can show your grandchildren what it looks like to live a life of patience. When you are patient with them, listen to them, and love them unconditionally, you give them a priceless gift.

Kindness

> Be kind to one another, compassionate, forgiving each other, just as God in Christ also has forgiven you.—Ephesians 4:32
>
> She opens her mouth in wisdom, And the teaching of kindness is on her tongue.—Proverbs 36:21

We can show our grandchildren what it looks like to live a life full of love and compassion, always lending a helping hand or offering a listening ear. By being kind to those around us, we improve their lives and reflect the light of Jesus Christ in this world.

We need to be intentional about showing kindness to our grandchildren. In a world that can be harsh and full of violence, our grandchildren need to see firsthand that there is another way to live. They need to know that they are loved unconditionally and belong to a community of people who gently guide them instead of pushing them away. This type of kindness, which comes directly from the Holy Spirit, is a beautiful offering we can make to our grandchildren.

Goodness

> Now for this very reason also, applying all diligence, in your faith supply moral excellence, and in your moral excellence, knowledge, and in your knowledge, self-control, and in your self-control, perseverance, and in your perseverance, godliness, and in your godliness, brotherly kindness, and in your brotherly kindness, love.—2 Peter 1:5-7

> *And concerning you, my brothers and sisters, I myself also am convinced that you yourselves are full of goodness, filled with all knowledge and able also to admonish one another.* —Romans 15:14

There's a similar theme in these two scriptures: goodness and knowledge. Goodness is consistently tied to learning and instruction (teaching). As I apply the fruit of goodness to grandparenting, it's apparent that when we pursue goodness, we share wisdom. Wisdom is good.

Never stop learning. Continue your pursuit of new things and new understanding so that you may show the fruit of goodness through the sharing of these things with your grandchildren.

Faithfulness

> *Know therefore that the Lord your God, He is God, the faithful God, who keeps His covenant and His faithfulness to a thousand generations for those who love Him and keep His commandments;* —Deuteronomy 7:9

> *His lord said to him, 'Well done, good and faithful servant; you have been faithful over a few things, I will make you ruler over many things. Enter into the joy of your lord.'*
> —Matthew 25:23, NKJV

Our faithful God is our trustworthy God. He keeps His covenants to a thousand generations. If that's not trustworthy, I don't know what is.

Faith is trust, and trust is faith. I know fully that trusting someone, including God, is one of the most challenging things we can do. The words of the Bible reassure us that God can be trusted.

When our time comes, we all want to hear those words, "Well done, good and faithful servant." Being faithful is one of the most important examples of faith you can offer your grandchildren.

Gentleness

> *but it should be the hidden person of the heart, with the imperishable quality of a gentle and quiet spirit, which is precious in the sight of God.—1 Peter 3:4*
>
> *Let your gentle spirit be known to all people. The Lord is near.—Philippians 4:5*

The world often glamorizes violence, aggression, and anger as signs of strength. But in reality, gentleness is not weakness – far from it! Instead, gentleness shows that you recognize your power in God and live in a way that focuses on using that power for good rather than for harm or destruction.

Jesus brought good through His gentle ways. He told stories to teach about Himself and His ways; He healed those who were sick; He blessed those who were hungry or had other needs even when they didn't deserve it. In all these things and more, we see examples of beauty and gentleness.

The Holy Spirit is known as the "gentle breeze." When you feel His presence in your life and allow Him to guide you, He will show you what gentleness means.

Self-Control

> *Everyone who competes in the games goes into strict training. They do it to get a crown that will not last, but we do it to get a crown*

that will last forever.
—*1 Corinthians 9:25, NIV*

Like a city that is broken into and without walls So is a person who has no self-control over his spirit.—*Proverbs 25:28*

Self-control is a critical aspect of the Christian life, and it's something that we can only receive from God. By relying on the Holy Spirit to give us this level of self-control, we can live our lives in a way that pleases God and brings him glory.

To have self-control, we need first to understand what motivates us - our sinful nature or our desire for approval from others. When we're living according to our sinful desires, we focus on ourselves and do whatever feels good at the moment. But when we put God above all else, we focus on pleasing him instead of ourselves. This is where self-control comes in - redirecting our desires away from selfishness and towards God, we can learn to control our thoughts, words, and actions.

When we practice being merciful, kind, generous, and compassionate toward those around us, we find peace within ourselves too. We are reminded of our worth and goodness.

with all humility and gentleness, with patience, bearing with one another in love, being diligent to keep the unity of the Spirit in the bond of peace.—*Ephesians 4:2-3*

The words from Ephesians are an essential, tidy little package where we can see many of the attributes of the Holy Spirit. It's a one-sentence guide to life. If you feel inclined, you can memorize it and meditate on it.

Pray

Father God, you are the perfect One. You show us what it means to live out the fruits of the Holy Spirit and how to live among one another.

The fruits sometimes seem like a long list of rules, but it's a relatively short guide to living our best lives. Thank you for giving us the gift of the Holy Spirit and the freedom to call on Him for the best ways to handle our worldly situations.

Lord, it can be overwhelming to think about how we are expected to live when so many others don't follow the same rules. Please help me remember that the Fruits of the Spirit are not rules but gifts. You have blessed me with them as a guide for living in harmony with others.

Lord, let me bless my grandchildren and all my family by producing the good fruit you've provided for joyful living.

In the name of Jesus, I pray, amen.

21

LEGACY

> *This will be written for the generation to come, That a people yet to be created may praise the Lord:—Psalm 102:18*

I love this scripture. It holds a guarantee, it holds promise, it holds prophecy, and it expects that we will carry out the Great Commission. Let's break it down. "This will be written . . . " are words that contain a guarantee. Similar to when people use phrases like "mark my words" or "just wait and see" to show that they are so confident that they want you to remember what they said. "For the generation to come, . . . " is a promise that generations will continue. There is more to come, and God isn't done yet. "That a people yet to be created . . . " is the prophecy of God's children, all of whom He already knows and has a plan for. That includes you, me, our children, and our children's children. "May praise the Lord." It's the calling set before us—praise and worship our Lord and Savior.

As grandparents, we can love and nurture our grandchildren and teach them about the love Jesus has for them and all the ways we have received blessings from God. Just as we speak about neighbors and relatives, we can share stories of our encounters with Jesus, the ways He has helped us, and how they, too, can have a relationship with Him.

The people yet to be created across the generations of our own families are the ones we secure the teachings of Christ with. As these conversations become more commonplace, our role in creating generations who will praise the Lord will reveal just how important it is for us to talk about God.

Be encouraging in your children's faith lives so that your grandchildren have a consistent teaching of God's word. That's not to say you have to attend the same church and keep your finger on the pulse of the faith walk of every person in the family. It simply means to be an example.

When you walk in faith, show the fruits of the Holy Spirit within your life, and live joyfully, you create a visual example of what life is like when you give it over to God. It's not perfect, but it is a reason to praise the Lord for His faithfulness and mercy.

There are many ways we can praise the Lord so that our grandchildren understand what it means—saying grace at meals, expressing gratitude when God answers a prayer, playing Christian music at home and singing along, reading devotionals to the little ones, and, of course, singing worship during church services.

My grandchildren express fears during storms or after having a bad dream; these are opportunities for us to assure them that God is protecting us. We can talk to Jesus about our fears and be thankful from a place of confidence that we are safe.

As an imperfect person with fears and concerns, I'm thankful I can rely on God to help curb my granddaughters' anxious thoughts. I have the authority of Jesus that brings peace not only to their young hearts but also to my mind. When everything turns out okay, we can rejoice and praise God for keeping us safe and wrapping His loving arms around us in our time of need.

This is an opportunity to impact generations of your blood. You can cut off negative generational cycles and create an all-new family line of Jesus followers. What a tremendous gift!

What will be recorded for your family line's future generations to reflect on? Will you follow God and share the good news of what He did for you and everyone you love, or will you step aside and watch life pass you by as your future generations remain suspended in a meaningless spiral?

From these words in Psalm 102:18, we know that a meaningless spiral is not what God had planned for us. Absolutely not. That scripture holds promise! Let it be recorded that a generation to come will praise the Lord! It was said that it would happen, and our calling is to ensure it comes to pass.

These verses are part of a prayer of a distressed person who had nothing and had been afflicted, yet he had faith that God would rebuild and show His glory to the people. The prayer ends in verse 28 with the following:

> *"The children of Your servants will continue, And their descendants will be established before You."* —Psalm 102:28

You can establish them before Him by praising God in your grandchildren's presence.

We know that we must build our houses on the solid rock of Jesus, and when you disciple your grandchildren, you establish them upon the rock where He guides them, protects them, and provides them eternal life in paradise. We can't *prove* anything by chance. It takes faithfulness, intention, and a deep desire for our descendants to have the best life possible.

Many portions of the Bible reference descendants, children, and children's children. Anytime something is mentioned so frequently in the Bible, we should pay attention because these are the things that God wants us to heed. If we follow His word relating to these things, we don't have to worry about what might become of our descendants or us.

Yes, we've taken a serious turn here, but we're talking about your grandchildren's place for eternity. We're talking about equipping them to handle the challenging moments life will throw at them, and we're talking about helping them understand where every blessing comes from and how their every need is met.

Life is difficult enough to deal with the here and now in our little worlds, much less concern ourselves with all our future generations. But if it's become apparent that no one in your *previous* generations concerned themselves with *your* future, I bet you recognize the importance and urgency of this message.

Everyone leaves a legacy. As we get older and start to think about our legacies, we must remember that the most important legacy we can leave is one of love, hope, and faith.

Even if you don't have children or grandchildren yet (or even if they're grown), you can still create a legacy of love that will stay with them their entire lives. All it takes is to remind them of how much you value them and show them how much they mean to you.

Write letters to them, even if they're just emails or text messages—tell them how proud you are of them and how much joy they bring into your life. Do this in birthday cards that they can look back on. Write down everything that makes them unique and why they mean so much to you! No one ever gets tired of hearing why they're so great. Unfortunately, most of us don't hear it enough.

Start a tradition of writing a special scripture on their birthday cards that speak to who they are as children of God. Keep a prayer journal that you give them as a graduation gift. Can you imagine how much impact that would have on them?

Give them photos of you with them and write a note on the back with a special message about that moment, along with scripture that might apply to it. Photos can speak volumes and evoke precious memories. Those moments that were captured, even if you captured them yourself (yay for selfies!), are part of the way you can ensure that your grandchildren know and remember your deep love for them.

Praying for your grandchildren in their presence has a similar effect as when they overhear someone speaking positively about them. They can listen in as you talk to God about them. I haven't personally experienced this too many times in my life, but I can tell you there is no more significant impact on self-worth than hearing what someone else says about you to God.

When you do your part in creating a loving environment for your grandchildren and valuing your children in front of them, the legacy you leave within them is astounding. It may be difficult for many GenXers to imagine because many of us likely haven't experienced this level of love and attention. But think about how you would feel. And then think about how it would feel to you if you did this for someone else.

What an incredible way to build hope in two people at once. It may seem awkward to even think about doing some of these things, much less acting on them. You probably worked on being more in touch with your emotions while raising your children. You recognized what you lacked, and you gave your children more.

Grandparenting doubles down on this. Honestly, I don't know how anyone gets through parenting without God. My faith life has been my peace. Now that I have grandchildren, my dependence on God is even more significant, and my understanding of His importance drives me to want my grandchildren to know these things, too.

Life is a lot easier when we have hope. The only place I've ever found hope is in Jesus. Even then, I've found it difficult to let my guard down to honestly hope with a childlike faith like we're meant to. When we've been jaded by life and haven't found much to place our hope in, that's a sign that we haven't yet placed it in Jesus.

Hope can't happen outside of Jesus Christ. God is love, Jesus is hope, and the Holy Spirit is peace. There's so much beauty in these aspects of our triune God that we can joyfully share with our grandchildren. You want the best for them; I promise you, God is the best.

The following scriptures on hope, faith, and legacy are an excellent way to learn more about God's heart for generations of His children. When you think about your legacy, read through these for inspiration not only for how vital your legacy is but also to understand what God has to say about it. He thinks generational faith is important enough to talk about in His book.

> *You, however, continue in the things you have learned and become convinced of, knowing from whom you have learned them, and that from childhood you have known the sacred writings which are able to give you the wisdom that leads to salvation through faith which is in Christ Jesus. —2 Timothy 3:14-15*

> *"Now this is the commandment, the statutes, and the judgments which the Lord your God has commanded me to teach you, so that you may do them in the land where you are going over to take possession of it, so that you, your son, and your grandson will fear the Lord your God, to keep all His statutes and His commandments which I command you, all the days of your life, and that your days may be prolonged.—Deuteronomy 6:1-2*

> *For I am mindful of the sincere faith within you, which first dwelled in your grandmother Lois and your mother Eunice, and I am sure*

> *that it is in you as well.* —2 *Timothy 1:5*
>
> *Even to your old age I will be the same, And even to your graying years I will carry you! I have done it, and I will bear you; And I will carry you and I will save you.* —*Isaiah 46:4*

The encouragement in Isaiah 46:4 is that God does not grow old with us. He does not wear out. He never changes; He provides us with everything we need, from the cradle to the grave. I find great hope in this.

There is nothing more important than leaving a legacy of faith. Grandparents have a sacred opportunity to share the love of the Lord with their children and grandchildren. Just as Paul reminded young Timothy of his spiritual heritage, grandparents are reminded of the importance of their spiritual legacy. What an encouragement for grandparents to rise up and actively share their faith in Christ.

Pray

Dear God, you have shown me that walking with you makes life better. I want that for my family, too.

I pray that I will outwardly exemplify your love to my grandchildren as I continue my path with you. I pray that they will see the joy and light within me that comes from knowing you and that they will choose you, too.

As I grow older and grow deeper in my faith, please let me remain focused on impacting my family to pursue a life built on the solid foundation of your faithfulness.

Thank you, Lord, for thoroughly preparing me to leave a legacy that points back to you.

In the name of your precious son, Jesus, I pray, amen.

22

HERITAGE

This kind of heritage is defined by beliefs and our family culture, not by where we were born or what language we speak. Our parents and grandparents have influenced us in ways they never imagined—and we influence our grandchildren in significant ways.

We can't change our heritage. The culture we were born into is permanent. Our family's values and traditions are deeply ingrained in us. Whether good or bad, we've received a heritage of identity that contributed to who we are today.

Heritage and legacy are very closely intertwined and yet very different. Heritage is what we received from previous generations. Legacy is what we're leaving for future generations. What we leave for future generations becomes their heritage. And the circle of heritage and legacy continues on and on.

Our heritage comes from our parents and our grandparents. They handed down what molded us, whether we accepted or denied those inheritances. We received them and may have held on to them for most of our lives, and during adulthood, we ended certain traditions, tendencies, or identities that no longer served us.

What kind of heritage have you received from your grandparents? If you're not sure, here are some things to consider:

What are the stories that you hear about your grandparents' lives?

What did they say about their childhoods?

How did their experiences shape them as people?

What kind of values did they pass down to you?

A lot of times, we don't think about our heritage because it seems so far away. But when we look back through our family tree and see how each generation has contributed something unique and valuable to the world—and left something behind for us to inherit—it helps us understand where we've come from and helps us make decisions about where we want to go next.

It makes sense then to think and apply the above questions to yourself.

What stories will your grandchildren hear about your life?

What have you shared about your childhood or life with your children or grandchildren?

How have your experiences shaped you?

What kind of values do you want to pass down to future generations?

If your heritage could have been better, you can change the course for future generations. Perhaps you've already begun this change with your children, which will also impact your grandchildren. If your heritage was ideal, you want to ensure those values remain for future generations of your family.

I'll add a few more questions:

How are you handling the digital/social media world?

What kind of digital footprint will your children and grandchildren inherit from you?

Are you handing down distraction and inattention?

Are you a good example of how to handle your digital presence?

Are you a good example of how to put people first?

Reflecting on these questions as they apply to you might help you make changes you never knew were needed. These questions may spark other aspects of your life you want to reflect on. It's always possible to change the narrative and make new choices. You can start anytime if you want to change traditions or improve your family's values. Nothing says that just because you've been doing something one way, you can't stop or change that when it no longer serves you well.

What you value is what will be repeated by your lineage. If your values aren't in alignment with what you want for your family, create new ones.

Our Boomer parents valued hard work, which meant they had less energy for us. Our generation loves hard work, but we also highly value family time. That's where the work-life balance conversation began. GenX decided we're not going to be so consumed with our jobs that it takes us away from our children. Boomers viewed work as a priority. GenX viewed our children as a priority. We continued the aspect of our heritage that demanded hard work, but we said no more to children being put on the back burner.

> *I have inherited Your testimonies forever, For they are the joy of my heart.*
> *—Psalm 119:111*

What kind of heritage will your grandchildren receive from you? Will you pass on your spiritual heritage—your faith walk? It seems like a simple question, but if you stop and think about it for a moment, it might not be as simple as you think.

Family traditions are great, and cultural values are essential to keep families rooted in their culture. Keep those things alive as long as they are fruitful and uplifting. But the real goal is to create generations of people who inherit eternal life in Heaven with God.

It's easy to assume that we'll pass on the things we value in our lives—the ones most important to us—but what if they aren't the things that will impact our children's and grandchildren's lives? What if they aren't things that will make an eternal impact? We can't begin to imagine what kind of world our grandchildren will live in when they're adults, so how can we possibly know what will matter most then?

> *It is the living who give thanks to You, as I do today; A father tells his sons about Your faithfulness.—Isaiah 38:19*

One thing we know will always matter is eternity. Passing down faith in God and knowing Jesus as Savior is a priceless inheritance for your grandchildren. As you've shared this truth with your children, and you share it with their children, the riches of this truth is magnified through generations.

When it comes to predicting the future, all that matters is eternity. It's not about the next thirty years; it's not even really about the entirety of our grandchildren's lives. It's about what one thing has true staying power that profoundly impacts every single generation that has ever lived, and that is to come: God.

> *When you cry out, let your collection of idols save you. But the wind will carry them all up, And a breath will take them away. But the one who takes refuge in Me will inherit the land And possess My holy mountain."—Isaiah 57:13*

I'm always in awe of the truth of this scripture from Isaiah. Idols will be easily blown away by the wind as light as a breath. When we seek God, we inherit His holy mountain. A mountain cannot be moved. A mountain remains for generations upon generations. God clearly shows us that He is the only one we should pursue.

Be careful not to pass down idols, as an inheritance of idols will not benefit your children and grandchildren. Whether those idols are work, addictions, or material things, now is a good time to do the work to focus on God. He is everlasting in the best way. Leaving an inheritance of idols to your children and grandchildren only brings them dissatisfaction and chasing after things that will never love them back.

> to *obtain* an inheritance *which is* imperishable, undefiled, and will not fade away, reserved in heaven for you,—*1 Peter 1:4*

When we pursue God, the inheritance becomes Heaven. No piece of property or possession you could pass down holds the value of a place in Heaven. Property and material things can be bought and sold or destroyed, but a place in Heaven is always secured for you and all who believe in Jesus as our Savior. We're talking about Paradise here, people. You can secure your place and make sure your family is coming with you.

> *Behold, children are a gift of the Lord, The fruit of the womb is a reward.—Psalm 127:3*

The Bible calls children the Lord's gift or "reward" for having faith in Him and following His ways. Other Bible versions use the word "heritage" in place of "gift." A reward speaks to the idea of something earned through hard work; it also implies something given as an incentive for doing good deeds or keeping one's word. As believers in Christ, we can rest assured that our Heavenly Father has blessed us with children because He sees children as His precious treasure!

Children are so important to God that they are *the* heritage from Him. His heritage is our fruitfulness, and that fruit is a reward. When he says we should be fruitful and multiply, this isn't just a command to populate the world.

God knows exactly what we need, and we need children. If there were no children, there'd be no generations and no one to leave an inheritance to. For us to receive the blessings of the Lord, we must accept our reward in the form of His heritage.

He created every one of us for His glory. But His glory results in our receiving a reward for obedience to his calling of having children. And then, our children have children, and the prize gets better and better!

> *Tell your sons about it, And have your sons tell their sons, And their sons the next generation.—Joel 1:3*

This verse from Joel reminds me of the song, 'Go Tell It on the Mountain.' I envision standing on a mountaintop shouting to all about the love and mercy of God, the salvation of Jesus Christ, and the incredible power of the Holy Spirit. I envision people stopping in their tracks to listen and receive the message, followed by cheers and singing.

I envision representatives from generation after generation sprinting to the top of the mountain to share this message and what a beautiful world this evolves into with each generation carrying out this commission.

GenX friends, we've created new generations greatly benefiting from our legacy of love. They are handing down that love and righteousness with the help of the faith in God that we nurtured. Keep moving forward in love because the rest of your years continue to change the course of the world. We're not done yet.

Pray

Dear God, I received some undesirable inheritances from generations before me. I want to change this and create a more positive and loving heritage for my children and grandchildren.

Please help me to make these changes by ending the things that don't add value to my identity. I have found my identity in you, and I want future generations to experience the fullness and peace that comes from that.

As I make these decisions, I ask the Holy Spirit to guide me, speaking to me about the places that need the most attention and how best to pursue them. I pray for the right way to communicate the changes if they need to be spoken. I pray for acceptance from my family for the end of what no longer serves us or future generations.

Thank you, Lord, for your unceasing love and guidance. Thank you for opening my heart to the new things you are doing within me.

In Jesus' name, I pray, amen.

23

TOP TIPS

Fortunately, we're not so old that we have to ask, "What do kids like to do these days?" Since many of you are grandparents with young children still at home, you're very in tune with great ways to entertain and play with your grandchildren.

In case you need some tips, there are a variety of things you can do with your grandkids to create memories for a lifetime. Here are just a few:

1. Take them on dates. Individual dates with your grandchildren are a great way to fill their buckets. Visit the park nearby, take them out for their favorite treat, go shopping and give them a $10 spending limit. You don't have to spend much money to make them feel special. Your time and full attention are all they need.

2. Make arts and crafts together. This is a great way to bond and wow them with your artsy knowledge! Show them that blending blue and red paint makes purple, or you can make cute bracelets out of pipe cleaners. Get a craft kit and keep the supplies in a plastic bin at your house so they can get creative whenever possible. Make some artwork for them to take home. Your grandchildren make art for you, so reciprocate the gesture and show them that you think they're special

by making a painting for them.

3. Play games together. Board games, card games, and games you make up are all great ways to have fun and learning opportunities. Alter the rules so the game is simpler, and be prepared to face fierce competition! Our oldest granddaughter is very competitive, to the point that she's let me win games because I'm terrible at them! Don't wait for them to ask you to play a game with them. Let them know you want to play a game and ask if they want to join you.

4. Read together. Reading to babies is a sweet way to bond. It encourages eye contact, they are soothed by the sound of your voice, and it builds a love of reading as they get older. With older children, take turns reading pages or even let them read to you. Some of our favorite moments have been when our granddaughters read to us.

5. Cook or bake together. You'd be surprised how much kids love being in the kitchen and helping. Let them be kitchen helpers when they're young, even if they get to pour ingredients into a bowl or set the table. When they're older, let them help with everything from cracking eggs, mixing ingredients, and, most importantly, taste testing the final product! Our oldest granddaughter loves to bake so much that my mom (her great-grandmother) gave her a well-loved cookbook for Christmas. It has her favorite Chocolate Chip Cookie recipe in it, and there's no way to describe the joy on her face when she opened that gift.

6. Share *your* favorite hobbies with them. My husband loves fishing and the outdoors, in general. He shared this with our granddaughter at a young age, and now she loves fishing with him. All the girls enjoy walking with him at the lake nearby because he points out various plants, birds, and trees. Don't assume that whatever your hobbies or passions are that the kids won't want to be involved. While you need to spend time doing things they like to do, it's just as vital that they get to experience activities you enjoy. Even if it's something they decide

they don't like to do, they'll still appreciate you sharing your interests with them and giving them a chance to get to know *you* better.

Toys

When it comes to toys, try to avoid the desire to jump too far ahead of their age. Age-appropriate toys are there for a reason. Buying an item they don't understand how to use will eventually end up in the donation box.

One thing we've learned is that simpler is better. Items that allow children to develop skills and use their imagination are, by far, the best ones. We're talking wood blocks, red solo cups, construction paper, and cardboard boxes.

You will be amazed at what children can do with these items. Our granddaughters have built castles, kingdoms, moats, rooms, and stores. They make money out of construction paper, warrior helmets out of cardboard boxes, and, of course, forts out of blankets.

While we built up our supply of toys to keep at our house, the things they've played with the most are the items that allow them the most creativity.

Other toys they've played with the most are a little push car, a small doll house with accessories, wood food that allows them to play restaurant (they love this as much as the cardboard and cups), sketch pads with crayons, colored pencils, and markers, and age-appropriate games.

Give them tools and let their imaginations create the experience. A ton of art supplies and some accessories allow children to explore, develop creativity, exercise their problem-solving skills, and gain confidence in their ability to create. All of this leads to confidence which is vital for developmental growth in children.

Experiences

Another way we've created some pretty awesome memories with our granddaughters is through dance parties and physical play. We put on some music and give each girl the floor to do their dance moves, they dance together, and we dance with them, and it's probably one of the best ways we connect with them.

Physical play is vital to connecting with them! Get down on the floor and play. When they're rowdy, wrestling, and crawling around, get down on their level and join in. They'll be surprised silly when you do, and you'll enjoy those sweet games of horsey and airplane that bring back your childhood memories.

Time in nature is a great way to provide a way to release their energy and learn about the world and connect to their environment. There are many ways to play, and learning through nature is vital. Kids need to have a space where they can get dirty, get messy, and just be themselves.

Here are some ideas for inexpensive ways to give your children's playtime a little boost:

1. Get them started with an indoor fort

2. Make a garden bed in the corner of your backyard where they can plant whatever they want.

3. Buy them some toys that encourage exploration: binoculars, magnifying glasses, and birdfeeders. Take a walk along a stream and talk about what you see. Collect pinecones, acorns, and other natural treasures.

4. Play in the dirt. Even if you don't have a backyard, there are plenty of ways to let your grandchildren play in nature. If you live near a park or forest, take them there—and even if you don't, there are plenty of opportunities for children to explore nature at home. Download an app for your nature adventure to incorporate technology and learning. Some apps can help you identify plants, trees, birds, and animals based on their sound.

5. Go on a scavenger hunt! Whether neighborhood-wide or just in your house, this is an excellent way for kids to learn about their environment by exploring it with their eyes open wide. Plus, it's fun!

6. Make up stories about the things around you! Kids love making up stories about things they see every day—it helps them understand the world better by giving it context through imagination. So when your child asks questions about what something is or why something happens, encourage them to make up an explanation that makes sense to them—they'll learn so much more than if you tell them what's going on!

Conversation

Make time to talk to your grandchildren. Turn off televisions and devices, grab a couple of juice boxes and some Pirate Booty, and visit with the littles. As soon as they can form sentences, have meaningful conversations with them. I promise this is the most effective way to build your relationship with them.

In the beginning, it'll be a little more one-sided: you asking questions and them giving simple two- to three-word answers. Over time, you'll find yourself listening as they share stories about their friends, their cat getting out of the house, and their fun date with their mom. Conversations with you will be some of their most treasured moments . . . especially as they get older.

Downtime

As important as it is to engage in playtime and connection, quiet time ranks pretty high, too. Watching a favorite show, having time on a device, or quietly playing alone with a toy are all vital to balancing each child's time with you.

Our goal is that our home is what they need it to be, depending on the day. On days that they are excited and ready to play, we do that. On days when they want to get under a blanket on the couch and watch a movie, we do that. We let them lead the way the visit will go. This is one of the significant aspects of What Happens at Nana's Stays at Nana's. They have rules, routines, and schedules when they're at home. When they're with us, they have autonomy.

If you don't live near your grandchildren and primarily connect with them through video calls, go on your walks so you can share stories with them about things you experience. Perhaps send them a magnifying glass or a list of nature goals they can do, and once they check everything off the list, you send them a gift card for an ice cream cone.

Hopefully, these tips spark other ideas in those dealing with the struggle of the distance between you and your grandchildren. Sharing a list of the activities you'd like to do with them on your next visit is a great way to create connections.

Whatever your situation, please remember that it doesn't cost much money to connect with your grandchildren. Their most valued treasure is the time you invest in them when they're with you. Children don't remember all the little trinkets and toys they're given over the years, but they sure do remember the shared moments and the memories made through meaningful connections.

Our grandchildren are old enough to write cards for us on birthdays or holidays. They always mention how much they love fishing or playing a particular game when we're together. They've never once told us how much they love it when we spend money on them.

The point of all this is that your grandchildren enjoy being with you. They have the most fun when you get on their level and play with them. Making them the center of your attention is the best gift you can give them that will never be thrown away. It will be part of your legacy that they will always cherish in their hearts.

24

PRAYERS FOR YOUR GRANDCHILDREN

The power of prayer has been proven for centuries. Whether you are a lifelong Christian or have never seen a Bible, you can pray for your grandchildren. Praying for your grandchildren is a vital way to show your love and support for them.

They are growing up in a world becoming increasingly hostile to Christian values and beliefs. It's essential to keep them grounded in their faith, so they can continue to make the world a better place through their actions as adults.

> *For this reason we also, since the day we heard about it, have not ceased praying for you and asking that you may be filled with the knowledge of His will in all spiritual wisdom and understanding,* —Colossians 1:9

Praying for your grandchildren provides them with spiritual guidance during difficult times, helping them find solutions when things seem impossible or hopeless. They'll be facing many challenges in their lives, and they'll need the help of a loving God if they're going to make it through. It's so easy to get caught up in the day-to-day tasks that we forget that our children and grandchildren are going through so much more than we ever did at their age, and they need us to intercede in prayer.

Praying for our grandchildren is something we should do every day. It doesn't have to be complicated or time-consuming; say a quick prayer when you see them or think about them throughout the day. You can even write down your prayers on paper and keep them somewhere close by so that you can refer back to them later when needed.

As they go out into the world and start making their own decisions, they need to know that someone is praying for them and rooting for them—and it might as well be their grandparents!

There are many different types of prayers that you can say or write for your grandchildren. Here are a few that can help you start a prayerful journey.

A simple prayer asking God to watch over and protect your grandchildren as they grow up. You might also ask God to help guide their decisions and strengthen them during difficult times:

> *Father God, I love my grandchild, and I know you love them even more. It's incredible to me that that's possible, and it's also so very comforting, Lord. Because of your love for your children, I know you are always with them. Lord, I pray for your hedge of protection around them, keeping them safe, healthy, and always knowing they are loved. Father, thank you for your never-ending protection and love. In Jesus' Name, I pray, amen.*

A prayer thanking God for the gift of your grandchildren. You could also thank Him for all He has done in their lives, including all the joys and blessings He has given you through them:

> *Lord, thank you for blessing me with the crown of grandchildren. You have been faithful to bless them with love and safety, which is so important to me. I'm having much fun getting to know their unique personalities and learning more about myself. What a beautiful new season of life you have blessed me with! I love you, Father, and I love my grandchildren. I pray they always know how much they are loved and valued. In the name of your precious Son, amen.*

A prayer asking God to bless your grandchildren with good health, happiness, and success in all areas of their lives:

> *Father in Heaven, hear my prayer of every blessing for my grandchildren. I pray they will have a lifetime of good health, happiness, and prosperity. I pray, Lord, that they will remain open to your Holy Spirit in understanding the plans you have for them. I place my hope in you for their future. Thank you, God, for the perfect path you've created for them. In Jesus' name, I pray, amen.*

A prayer specifically for one of your grandchildren who may be having a tough time. This could be a prayer for healing from an illness, comfort during a difficult time, or strength to deal with whatever challenges they face:

> *Lord, I come to you desperate and faithful. I know you are in control, yet I'm giving in to feelings of helplessness and fear. Forgive me, Father, for reacting outside of trust. I pray for renewed strength as I lay my concerns at your feet. Lord, I lift (name of the grandchild) up in faith that you will heal/comfort/cause to rise during this time. It breaks my heart to know they are hurting;*

my love can only do so much for them. You are the One True Healer, Great Counselor, Mighty God who knows our every need and delivers us from our pain and illness. Thank you, Father, for your healing and guidance. I love you. In the name of Jesus, I pray, amen.

Praying for your grandchildren is a great way to stay connected to them and help them grow in their faith. Try setting aside time to say or write prayers for them each day or week. You could even start a Prayer Journal where you write down your prayers for them and how God answered them. This is a unique way to document your faith journey and the progress of your grandchildren's lives.

Consider also praying *with* them. When my grandchildren are with me, I sometimes ask them if there is anything I can pray about with them. Then we talk to God together. We've developed a more profound bond because we share our faith in life. We also do prayer before bed when they have sleepovers. They are active in their prayer life because they've been raised to know Jesus and pray regularly. No words could convey how comforting and joyful it is to listen to these precious children talk to God.

When you pray for your grandchildren, it's not just about connecting with them—it's also about connecting with yourself. You may be asking God to help guide your grandchildren through life, but in doing so, you're also asking God to guide YOU through life!

Praying for your grandchildren reminds us of the importance of remaining true to our values and what we want our legacy to be. When we remain in the habit of relying on God, that helps us to build trust in God and rely on His faithfulness which grows our faith.

Our prayer life is the single most important part of our spiritual growth and, for many of us, it often becomes the first thing we abandon in the busyness and stress of life. GenX is used to being self-sufficient and in control of our situations. It may take us more effort to create the habit of prayer.

You can pray for spiritual growth in your grandchildren's lives as well. Asking God to strengthen your grandchildren's development in their relationship with Him naturally results in a strong relationship between you and God.

You can also pray that they will be able to develop good relationships with others who are important to them so that they will feel loved and supported by those around them. Praying for your grandchildren means asking God to ensure they have everything they need to grow up into healthy adults who can care for themselves without worrying about anything else besides being happy with who they are and what they do each day.

Prayer is one of the most beautiful gifts we have received as children of God.

When you pray for your grandchildren, you open to a deep connection with our Creator. You're acknowledging that you don't have to face everything alone, which most of us desperately need at some point in our lives.

When we feel connected to God, we feel loved.

We acknowledge that things exist outside our experience and understanding when we pray. We recognize there is more than we can see or understand right here and now. That's why prayer helps us feel more grounded in our faith walk.

> *Now in the same way the Spirit also helps our weakness; for we do not know what to pray for as we should, but the Spirit Himself intercedes for us with groanings too deep for words;* —Romans 8:26

Praying for your grandchildren is essential because you want them to make good decisions and stay on the right path regarding their faith. Praying for them is one way that you can help guide them through their journeys as Christians.

Whether you pray out loud, in private, through journal entries, or with them, they will appreciate your love and support as they face the challenges of growing up in this world!

Prayer is powerful.

Pray

Lord, I confess that sometimes it's difficult for me to pray. Often I don't know what to say, some days, I feel like I don't deserve to pray, and other times, it's not the first thing on my mind.

Forgive me for the time I've lost when I could have been communicating with you, deepening my relationship with you, and laying my concerns at your feet.

I want to share this beautiful step of faith with my grandchildren to show them that you are always there, willing to listen to them at any time.

Father, please send your Holy Spirit to help me remember to pray to you first. I ask your Holy Spirit to intercede when I cannot find the words or feel inadequate. As your child, I know you love me, and you love hearing from me.

With your help, I can be a prayerful grandparent, blessing my grandchildren daily.

In the name of Jesus, I pray, amen.

My Prayer for You

Lord, bless your precious child who is reading this right now. Her heart for her grandchildren is full of love and adoration. Guide her to find fullness in her heart for you, Lord. As she navigates this new life donning the crown of grandchildren, bless her with the anointing of the Fruits of the Holy Spirit. Rain down love, joy, peace, patience, kindness, goodness, faithfulness, gentleness, and self-control over her in the way that only you can. These fruits are good because you are good, Father. Bless her, keep her, and shine your light on her so that she can reflect your light to others. In the name of our Savior, Jesus Christ, I pray, amen.

About the Author

Tonya Masters Ludwig is a creative using her gift for writing, entrepreneurship, and inventing. Her most profound inspiration is found in her grandchildren. After over a decade of grandparenting as a member of GenX, she recognized there were many differences for this generation.

In addition to her work as an author, Tonya is also devoted to literacy for individuals with special needs. She provides literacy mentoring through The Next Chapter Book Clubs, providing social reading experiences for adults with developmental disabilities. When she isn't writing, Tonya spends her time with her family — especially the grands — and being a lifelong learner of God, entrepreneurship, and health and wellness issues.

For more grandparenting, entrepreneurship, and following my writing journey, follow me on Instagram: @tonyamastersludwig or Facebook: Tonya Masters Ludwig

Visit my website at www.tonyamastersludwig.com

For more information on setting healthy boundaries and handling family dynamics, follow my daughter on Instagram, Facebook, and TikTok: @kailahwhite

To view and purchase Eliza's Encouraging Pillows, visit her store at www.sowathome.com

Made in the USA
Las Vegas, NV
21 January 2023